Pelican Books
The School Debate

Adam Hopkins has divided his career between
teaching, journalism and more personal writing.
Spells working for the British Council and the
Polytechnic of Central London have alternated with
newspaper work, mostly with *The Sunday Times*.
He was *Sunday Times* education correspondent from
1975 to 1977. Today he writes on education and
travel for a variety of journals. A travel book,
Crete; its past, present and people, was published in
1977. His poetry has appeared in magazines and has
been heard on B.B.C. radio. Born in 1939, he was
educated at Winchester College, Western Reserve
Academy, Ohio, and at King's College, Cambridge.
He is married and has two sons at maintained
schools.

Adam Hopkins

The School Debate

Penguin Books

Penguin Books Ltd, Harmondsworth,
Middlesex, England
Penguin Books, 625 Madison Avenue,
New York, New York 10022, U.S.A.
Penguin Books Australia Ltd, Ringwood,
Victoria, Australia
Penguin Books Canada Ltd, 2801 John Street,
Markham, Ontario, Canada L3R 1B4
Penguin Books (N.Z.) Ltd, 182–190 Wairau Road,
Auckland 10, New Zealand

First published 1978

Made and printed in Great Britain by
Cox & Wyman Ltd, London, Reading and Fakenham
Set in Intertype Times

For my wife, Margaret, who sees it all first hand

Contents

Foreword

The School Debate surrounds us on all sides. The past, present and future of our educational system and the welfare of the millions of children caught up in it are eagerly discussed in public and in private. But it is seldom possible to get a clear idea of what is going on. Standing as if at the centre of a battlefield, the observer may for a moment make out some happening in the most precise detail. Meanwhile the rest is obscured by cannon smoke. Suddenly the smoke lifts in a new quarter, revealing more of the action. No sooner has that happened than previously clear vistas fill up again with smoke.

This book is an attempt to resolve the difficulty by looking at the main issues of the School Debate against the background of what actually happens in schools from day to day. My hope is to offer the reader enough information and enough understanding of contemporary thought on education to enable him to make some sense of future developments, however confusing they seem in isolation.

Public debate has grown increasingly intense since about 1969, the year when the first of the conservative Black Papers on education was published. It took a new and more formal turn in October 1976 when James Callaghan drew together in a much publicized prime ministerial speech at Ruskin College, Oxford, many of the main themes of contemporary anxiety – modern teaching methods, the question of standards, the problem of what children should learn, the relationship between school and the economy and many more. This was followed by a series of nine, set-piece, regional debates, which in their turn were accompanied by much discussion in the press and on television and radio. From this there emerged a generally heightened public consciousness, some shifts of direction in the schools themselves and one or two new departures, more impressive in principle than practice, in national policy. Bigger changes may well lie in the future. Meanwhile the School Debate goes on. All this is the subject matter of the present volume. The book opens with a chapter on comprehensive reorganization, a question that has been somewhat swept aside in the past year or two. Yet it is fundamental to everything else; and the direction of events is very different from the popular perception of what is happening. This chapter is followed, by way of briefing for the debate itself, by an essay on modern developments inside school and another on the increasingly hostile reaction to them. Then come the five central issues of what was called the Great Debate – the curriculum, school and work, standards and their assessment, the teachers and the question of who should control the system. To these I have added two more that were left out – the problem of race in the inner cities and school closures in country districts. Together, these topics occupy chapters four and five. The last chapter is a brief checklist of policy developments.

The difficulties in writing about education are immense. Consider, for a moment, a single class in school, the individual differences of the children, the complexities of personal relationship, the range of subject matter, the range of differences in what is actually learned, the differences between one day and another, one teacher and another, one year and another. Multiply those complexities by ten or twenty till you have a primary school, by thirty or forty till you have a secondary school. Multiply and multiply till you have all the schools in England and Wales – and you will have some idea of the difficulties in making a valid general statement. Yet one cannot proceed at all without the help of general statements. All those who write about education must therefore offer their work humbly – and must themselves proceed like early navigators, continually in fear of falling off the edge.

The names of many of those who have helped me in the preparation of this book figure in the text in their own right. To them I offer the gratitude of a journalist for their great kindness and patience in answering multitudinous questions. I should like to thank four others whose names do not appear: Hugh Jones, headmaster of Gwernyfed High School, Powys; Stephen Sharp, assistant education officer, Birmingham; Margaret Nash, deputy head of Langbourne Primary School in London and Bob Gledhill of Westminster City School, also in London. My thanks to the editors of the *Vole*, *The Times Educational Supplement* and *The Sunday Times*, all of whom have given me free rein with information originally collected on their behalf. The greatest thanks of all must go to two people with whom I have had the opportunity in recent years to share ideas on education and from whom, if I have paid attention, I hope I have learned something of what is happening. These are Peter Newsam, education officer of the Inner London Education Authority, and Anne Sofer, formerly secretary of the National Association of Governors and Managers, now an elected member of the I.L.E.A. And special thanks to Pattie Ward who typed away through thick and thin.

1. Not so comprehensive

In the quarter century before 18 October 1976 – the day when James Callaghan, as Labour Prime Minister, declared an official interest in the internal workings of education – the main educational issue was whether or not we should 'go comprehensive'. Today's anxieties are increasingly bound up with what goes on inside the schools. But the success or failure of the attempt to reform the system lies behind all of them, and no consideration of what is happening in education today can be of worth unless it takes the ideology and practicalities of this struggle into account. From the end of the Second World War, with constantly gathering volume, argument over the question of the comprehensives went parallel with a scramble to build enough schools for the children of the post-war baby boom. In the words of a much meditated Government Green Paper[1] published in 1977, this was a period when the issues of building and secondary reorganization had 'overshadowed all education debate and education planning'. Now things were different, said the Green Paper. The school population was about to shrink; and reorganization was 'largely accomplished'.

The drop in the number of school children is one of the most important subjects with which this book will be concerned. But the second assertion, as I hope to show in the following pages, was simply not true. Many of the schools described as comprehensive were still not enormously different in intellectual or social terms from the 'secondary moderns' they replaced. In almost one third of the 104 local education authorities in England and Wales, the struggle to eliminate selection was continuing with a good deal of bitterness and not much prospect of an early end. Even more important, there was a lively chance that any Conservative administration would introduce new forms of selection. This meant that the question of comprehensive reorganization remained central, despite the efforts of Mr Callaghan's government to persuade us that the tide of reform was irreversible.

The original idea behind the comprehensive movement was to end disparities in education which mirrored those in society at large. This social idealism, most often expressed today as a desire for equality of opportunity, was strong among radical teachers in the 1920s and 1930s and reached an early peak during the Second World War. This was a time when the children of well-to-do families went to public or fee-paying grammar schools and there was little opportunity for anybody else. Theoretically there existed a ladder of ability up which anybody bright enough could climb, winning a free place to secondary school and after that, perhaps, a scholarship to university. In practice the vast majority of pupils received only elementary education, ending at fourteen. As late as 1943 a mere 9.5 per cent of elementary pupils went on to secondary school. But at about this time many people believed that if secondary education were to be made available to all, then this should be done in a way that healed divisions rather than exacerbated them. A Government White Paper of 1943 said roundly that social unity within the education system . . . would open the way to a more closely knit society'.

Unfortunately for the aspirations of the early supporters of comprehensive education, other, more powerful, forces, acting equally in the name of enlightenment, were pulling in the opposite direction. The theory which triumphed held that while it was monstrous to divide children according to their *social* origins, they would get a more effective education if they were divided according to *ability*. Dr I. G. K. Fenwick in his recent study of comprehensive reorganization[2] has shown how psychologists, among them the late Sir Cyril Burt (some of whose work has recently and controversially been called in question), were at that time emerging as a dominant cadre in educational research. Their apparently scientific approach appeared a guarantee of objectivity; and the over-simplified picture which laymen formed from their work was of a population in which each individual possessed an innate and unvarying level of intelligence. If this was so, then segregation, allowing different schools to specialize in the needs of a particular ability band, was a perfectly logical consequence. Belief in specialization echoes and re-echoes through the major educational reports of the twenties, thirties and forties. Here are the main examples, assembled by Dr Fenwick.

By the time that the age of eleven or twelve has been reached, children have given some indication of difference in interest and abilities sufficient to make it possible and desirable to cater for them by means of schools of varying types ...

(From the Hadow Report, 1926)

We were informed that, with a few exceptions, it is possible at a very early age to predict with some degree of accuracy the ultimate level of a child's intellectual power, but this is true only of general intelligence and does not hold good in respect of specific aptitudes or interests ... In general, minor differences, which were hardly noticeable in the infant school, will be distinctly observable in the primary schools, and by the age of eleven will have increased so much that it will no longer be sufficient to sort out different children into different classes. Different children, by the age of eleven, if justice is to be done to their varying capabilities, require types of education varying in certain important respects.

(From the Spens Report, 1938)

The Norwood Report, 1943, took this to its most extreme in proposing three types of school for differing types of mind: grammar schools for those 'interested in learning for its own sake'; technical schools for those 'whose interests or abilities lay markedly in the field of applied science or applied art'; and a third type of school for the larger number whose minds dealt 'more easily with concrete things than with ideas'.

The Education Act of the following year – the 1944 Education Act, to which all argument so frequently returns – established the principle of free, compulsory secondary education for all. It also provided for the raising of the school leaving age to fifteen (implemented in 1947) and then to sixteen (finally and

controversially achieved, after many delays, in 1972). This expansion of secondary education offered greater opportunities
for more people than ever before, a fact which is now sometimes obscured by the inequities which arose through the distribution of those opportunities. For though the Act said only
that the schools should offer children 'such variety of instruction as may be desirable in view of their different ages, abilities
and aptitudes' – a form of words which could have allowed or
even encouraged the immediate growth of comprehensives – the
scheme adopted was in fact the tripartite division into grammar,
technical, and modern school proposed in the Norwood Report.
The technical schools never became properly established and so
the system polarized into grammar and secondary modern.
There was meant to be 'parity of esteem' between the two kinds
of school, but this was utterly fictitious. Children were selected
for grammar school, in numbers which varied considerably
from one area to another, on the basis of assessment at eleven-
plus. The method of assessment varied widely but in the early
days there was a heavy reliance on I.Q. tests since these were
supposedly objective. Though the Act enshrined the principle of
parental choice, there was in fact little choice except for those
whose children performed well in I.Q. tests.

During the vital years from 1945 to 1951, while this system
was becoming established, the leaders of the ruling Labour
party gave the impression of being scarcely aware of the
alternative option of comprehensive schooling. The provision
of universal secondary education seemed in itself to be
sufficient gain. But throughout these early years one or two
M.P.s with an interest in education, and above all the National
Association of Labour Teachers, banged away at the theme of
equality of opportunity and a unified society. One of the clear-
est expressions of the ideology which inspired them came from
Margaret Cole in 1952:[3]

I do not believe that any socialist can call any education system
socialist or even democratic which does not bring children together
in a common school life, whatever their parents' income or previous
history.

This echoed, in more egalitarian language, the democratic intentions long before built into American secondary education and made explicit in a U.S. government report of 1918:[4] that secondary education should be directed towards developing, among all students in a community, 'a sense of common interests and social solidarity'. The American Dream was still sufficiently intact for American ideals to seem acceptable without much questioning. Later, as we shall see, the comprehensive issue became far more complex; but in the early post-war years in Britain it appeared to many radical reformers that a nation which had endured five years of anguish in unquestioning unity, could now throw off the worst excesses of a crippling class structure. Comprehensive education could be a powerful regenerative force. But this was only possible, so Margaret Cole, for one, suggested, if the comprehensive system was complete and flawless, unspotted even by minimal segregation. For the time being, she wrote, several different systems would have to coexist. In the end it was an issue on which compromise was simply not possible.

The issue of the indivisibility of comprehensive education remains to this day deeply contentious; for the equal and opposite claim that comprehensive and selective schools can coexist lies at the heart of present Conservative policy.

Paradoxically, some of the earliest comprehensives were initiated by Conservative local authorities. The comprehensive school at Tadcaster in the West Riding is a good example. It was set up in a solidly Conservative area, despite Labour suspicions, and with a bishop, then as now, as chairman of its board of governors. This kind of thing generally happened in sparsely populated, rural areas, most of them under Tory control, simply because it was easier to bring all secondary pupils together to a single omnibus school, offering on one site the kind of variety demanded by the 1944 Act. That Conservative councils did this, lent a good deal of credibility to the comprehensive movement. But right up into the 1960s, comprehensives were generally viewed as experimental and, outside the rural areas, they were established mainly in places such as new towns, where there were no grammar schools whose status would have to be changed if any genuinely non-selective scheme were introduced. This was the norm during the thirteen years of Tory national government from 1951 to 1964. Wherever Labour authorities put forward anything approaching a system-wide scheme – as happened during this period in Birmingham, Manchester and London – there was trouble over the status of individual grammar schools and in the end only diluted schemes were introduced, with considerable consequences for the future. Birmingham still retains some grammar schools; Manchester and London had to wait till 1977 for their first year of all-comprehensive secondary entry.

From the reformist point of view this was the waste of an opportunity to make the change cleanly. At the same time it illustrated the difficulties that flowed from the lack of a clear national policy. This point was made again, and another opportunity missed, when the school leaving age was raised in 1972. ROSLA (as it is often called) meant an expansion in the numbers at school and much new building was done as a result. But it was often done in isolation, without any thought of how it could promote comprehensive reform. The extra children who would be staying on were either in comprehensives already or in secondary moderns. Now the secondary moderns were extended, mainly by the addition of expensive new workshops for craft subjects. But all of these schools were soon to house 'comprehensive' pupils of all abilities. What the administrators *should* have built, as we can now see with hindsight, were the science laboratories so grossly lacking in comprehensive schools today.

Alternatively, the primary leaving age could have been raised to twelve as the Plowden Report[5] on primary schools had recommended. This would have created enough room in the secondary schools and meant that any necessary building could have been transferred to the cheaper, primary end. It would also, by the same token, have meant an enormous increase in the number of pupils in comprehensives. For the primary schools, though few people remember this, are of course comprehensive.

Administratively, those in authority behaved for two decades and more as if they were working towards a permanent mixed system, part comprehensive, part selective.

During these years of experiment, however, the 'pure' comprehensive ideal was making steady progress. It won substantial support from the middle classes, for the simple reason that they were no longer able to extract their children from the hurly-burly by paying grammar school fees. Grammar school places were now free and middle-class children had to compete for them like everybody else. Middle-class parents did not like it when their children failed the eleven-plus and were 'condemned', so they thought, to the secondary moderns. The Labour party was also readying itself to adopt a 'pure' comprehensive programme. This became official policy in 1951 and was restated, a good deal more emphatically, in 1959. The teachers' unions were coming round as well. The National Union of Teachers, by far the biggest of them, had endorsed 'multilateral' education, though only on an experimental basis, in 1943. By 1964, in giving evidence to the Plowden Committee on primary education, it said that it would prefer to see all local authorities who were eliminating selection by ability 'adopt the fully comprehensive school as the model for the future'. N.U.T. leaders claim that this support helped the Labour party to come out strongly for comprehensive education in the election that led to its narrow win in 1964. Labour knew that N.U.T. members, at least, would not fight them in the schools. This knowledge, no doubt, also made it easier for Anthony Crosland, as Secretary of State for Education, to issue his famous circular 10/65 the following year. This requested local authorities which had not already done so, to submit proposals for comprehensive reorganization by July 1965. Though the circular was quite specifically a request and not an order, the result was an enormous upsurge in the number of all-through comprehensive systems proposed by local authorities and sanctioned – as was necessary under the 1944 Act – by central government.

But by now the main focus of the comprehensive argument had shifted a good deal. Whereas the original drive was largely a social one, it had now become apparent that a divided education system was offering nothing like equality of educational opportunity. For a start, the variations in the number of grammar school places meant that many children who would have won grammar school entry if they had lived, say, in the south-east or London, would not get them if they lived in the north. There were grammar places for 31·7 per cent in London and the south-east, for 22·4 per cent in the north, for 18·9 per cent in the south and for even less in some smaller areas considered individually. This implied an enormous wastage of talent. Selection itself was unreliable. Findings published by the National Foundation for Educational Research in 1957[6] showed that about 10 per cent of children were wrongly placed each year – that is to say, about 78,000 children in 1955. Evidence assembled by such researchers as J. W. B. Douglas in his important and moving study *The Home and the School*[7] made it quite clear that the wastage was greatest among children of manual working-class parents. But, equally, many children accepted into grammar schools languished in the academic atmosphere, became demoralized and dropped out early. All this led to a wave of revulsion against I.Q. tests, which were now downgraded in the selection process by many local authorities. Today we seem to be moving into a 'sociological' age, leaving the 'psychological' behind. Concern has shifted, this time towards the possibility of wastage of talent and inequality of opportunity *inside* the comprehensive school. The topic will be taken up in following chapters; but in the early days simply to introduce schools called 'comprehensive' and theoretically catering for children of all abilities seemed to many reformers to be a sufficient response. The battle was mainly structural.

Another strand in the cat's-cradle of comprehensive ideology was a fear that the loss of talent implicit in a divided educational system would prevent Britain from moving forward into a technological world. This theme was strongly argued by Caroline Benn and Brian Simon in their book *Half Way There*[8] – the key account of comprehensive school reform from the viewpoint of its adherents.

Benn and Simon were unusual in that they were arguing at a high political level for a new *kind* of education. There was plentiful evidence, they wrote, that 'the traditional academic school is too limited and too inflexible in outlook to provide the form of secondary education now needed . . .'. They wanted an education which was related more firmly to the realities of the modern world, while being fully accessible to all. Some of the implications of this thinking are explored in the next chapter. But it is important to realize that many Labour spokesmen took a different view.

Sir Harold Wilson, for instance, shared Benn and Simon's enthusiasm for technology and as Labour leader he established a neat theoretical conjunction between a vibrant economy, equality of educational opportunity, the comprehensives and technological development. He contrasted all this with the prevailing system of 'educational apartheid'.[9] But he also claimed, and continued to claim till as late as 1970, that he was advocating something closer to grammar school education for all. This had actually been spelled out in a House of Commons motion in 1965 preceding the issue of circular 10/65. Reorganization on comprehensive lines, the motion said, 'will preserve all that is valuable in grammar school education for those children who now receive it and make it available to more children . . .'.

There have always been two differing versions inside the Labour movement of what is meant to be happening. One is broadly egalitarian – the Benn and Simon view. The other, full of respect for self-improvement and memories of Aneurin Bevan in the public library of Tredegar, is far more traditional. It is highly significant that as Mr Callaghan's Great Debate rolled on, the Labour government of 1977 was once again stressing the wording of the 1965 motion with its reference to grammar school ideas.[10]

Out and out resistance to comprehensive reorganization began to build surprisingly late. From the very beginning there had been mutterings about size and 'education factories' – it was officially reckoned that some 1300 pupils were necessary in an eleven-to-eighteen school to support a sixth form with a satisfactory range of subjects. There had been sharp local rows, some of them spectacular, when individual grammar schools were threatened. But shortly after the issue of circular 10/65, the number and ferocity of these rows increased enormously; and the Conservative party began to lend support to grammar school campaigners on a nation-wide basis. Even if it meant a denial of opportunity to those in secondary moderns, the cry of 'Save our School' had a fine populist ring – David against the Goliath of socialist bureacracy. Because of what they saw as the need to defend the grammar school, the mood among Conservatives became more and more anti-comprehensive. The charge of 'levelling down' was frequently heard. In 1969, the first Black Paper[11] warned that traditional grammar school values were being jettisoned. The critics of reform argued, with enormous elaboration, that comprehensives scored fewer exam successes than grammar and secondary modern schools together. (The debate on this point has continued obsessively ever since. See 'Standards', Chapter Four.) There was also great anxiety about the fate of the most-able children. Comprehensive supporters argued that theirs was the only framework within which *all* children had a chance of making the most of their abilities; critics maintained that the talents of the ablest, our most precious national asset, were being squandered for ideology's sake.

By 1970, when the Conservatives returned to office, it was Mrs Margaret Thatcher who was in charge of educational policy; and she, according to a former colleague,[12] 'was "not disposed to listen" to the unalloyed liberalism of the education service'. Within days she had withdrawn the Crosland circular with its official backing for the comprehensives.

As Labour spokesmen frequently observe, this led to scarcely any slowing down in the number of schools either going comprehensive, or starting up as comprehensives, every year. Plans already underway were usually completed; many new plans were submitted and approved. But according to Benn and Simon there was one highly significant change: 'The new policy was that local authorities should be free to be comprehensive or selective *or both at once*' (my italics). This meant that in a higher proportion of schemes approved under Mrs Thatcher, grammar schools were allowed to survive alongside schools which were nominally comprehensive. A document produced by the Campaign for Comprehensive Education, in December 1977[13] claimed that in 1974 over half the country's so-called comprehensives had selective schools in their immediate areas. 'Today it is likely to be only very little less.' In 1975, a survey in *The Times Educational Supplement* had found that there were still grammar schools in 78 of 104 local education authority areas in England and Wales. These took about 9·5 per cent of children instead of the 20 per cent taken by grammar schools in the early 1960s. In early 1978, 70 authorities still had some grammar schools. The implication was clear. Coexistence, though diminishing quite rapidly, was still deeply embedded and would remain a factor until comprehensive education became the universal pattern. Yet Benn and Simon claim[14] that it is coexistence which 'is, and always has been, the greatest threat to comprehensive reform'.

The arguments here depend not simply on the principles of natural justice – as advanced by Margaret Cole – but also on a demonstration of the practical difficulties involved in any half-way solution. Reporting in 1970, the Public Schools Commission had remarked that 'grammar schools ... cannot be combined with a comprehensive system ... We must choose which we want.' This became the text for a report on research into coexistence undertaken by Caroline Benn for the N.U.T. and the Campaign for Comprehensive Education. (She was research officer for the latter.) This was published in 1975, and though it was based on a relatively small sample, it seemed to show beyond all doubt that the great majority of comprehensives which had to coexist with grammar schools felt that they suffered adverse consequences. The most serious of these was a lowering in the number of high-ability pupils and an increase in the number of lower-ability pupils. (This is known as 'creaming'; whenever it occurs, exam results are distorted to the disfavour of the comprehensive sector, a matter to which I will return in Chapter Four.) Eighty-eight per cent of coexisting schools in the survey were affected by creaming. Eighty-six per cent felt they were affected by a lower level of esteem in the community. Seventy-six per cent said that coexistence diminished the number of middle-class pupils and increased the proportion of working-class pupils. There were more problem children, lower staff morale, greater difficulty in hiring specialist staff, and greater difficulty – because of the shortage of pupils staying on – in running reasonably economic courses at a higher level.

How serious the effects of creaming could become was illustrated by the plight of Inner London during the 1970s. The early London comprehensives did well. Because the schools were few, each attracted talented children whose parents positively preferred the comprehensives to the grammar schools. But when the remaining secondary moderns went comprehensive, the bright children outside grammar schools became more and more thinly spread. The exam results of the old-established comprehensives began to plummet and a fact which had previously been obscured became ominously plain – comprehensives could not be comprehensive until the grammar children came in too.

It is hard, in fact, to see that creamed comprehensive schools are very much better off in terms of intake than the secondary moderns they were meant to replace. It is findings such as those of Caroline Benn that undermine the effect of the government's bland statement during 1977 that four-fifths of children of the appropriate age-group were now being educated in comprehensive schools. When is a comprehensive not a comprehensive? There has been much hair-splitting on this point but it seems frankly absurd to believe that any noticeably creamed school is comprehensive in more than a superficial sense. The government's statement emerges as just one more in a long sequence of unrealistic claims on this subject. There are two rival explanations for this lack of realism. One is that these figures are intended as self-fulfilling prophecies, likely to persuade opponents that reform has gone so far they might as well acquiesce. The other, the conspiracy theory, holds that the figures are produced to mollify ministers by civil servants opposed to drastic change.

Whichever is correct, the problem facing Labour when it returned to power in 1974 was far greater than politicians or administrators were prepared to admit. The incoming Secretary of State immediately issued a circular withdrawing Mrs Thatcher's and reaffirming the government's intention to press on towards complete reorganization. But by now about a third of all local authorities seemed to have decided to hold out in some areas at least. Some half a dozen were openly defiant and in one, Tameside, on the outskirts of Manchester, a Tory council, elected in the spring of 1976, threw out a plan for comprehensive reorganization, though it was due to take place that very autumn. Educational liberals, teachers' unions and government were aghast. The government, as was its right in law, brought an action against Tameside council for behaving 'unreasonably'. But after several rounds of litigation, the Law Lords found for Tameside and left the government looking very silly.

While all this was going on, the government was struggling to enact a new Bill giving it the powers it needed to finish the long job of reorganization. This measure was bitterly resisted in Parliament but finally became law late in 1976.

But finishing the job was not to prove so simple. In several important respects the new Act followed the pattern of a Bill introduced for the same purpose in 1970 but which was delayed in its committee stage and lapsed later that year when Labour fell. The new Act, just as intended in the lapsed Bill, gave the Secretary of State power to conduct a running dog-fight with any authority she cared to challenge (Shirley Williams was now in the chair following short periods of occupation by Reg Prentice and Fred Mulley). The technical provisions of the new law meant that in the end the government was bound to win. But the process would take time and there seemed every prospect that the local authorities would be able to hold out till the next general election, due in 1979 at the latest. Meanwhile, Norman

St John-Stevas, as the Conservatives' Shadow Education Secretary, was both promising to repeal the Act if the Conservatives won, and actively advising in tactics of resistance. One after another, the rebellious authorities began to submit plans for reorganization – as they were now obliged to do by Mrs Williams – but these tended to be comprehensive on paper rather than in their intended effect. The most common tactic was an attempt to preserve the existing grammar schools as eleven-to-eighteen-comprehensives and to keep the secondary moderns as eleven-to-sixteen-schools. Prestige and sixth forms would thus remain with the former grammar schools and wherever parental choice was allowed, it was likely that those families who were already best informed – those, in other words, which produced the normal clientele of grammar schools – would be likely to take a disproportionate number of places in the former grammar schools. Inevitably, therefore, the Secretary of State was obliged to reject a number of these plans and ask the local authorities to try again. And so the dance continued, with the government reportedly reluctant to use the sanction of prosecution enshrined in the new Education Act.

Tameside, however, added a special refinement by conducting a poll which purported to show that the general public, and even the mass of teachers, were in favour of keeping the local grammar schools. Few on the Labour side were much impressed by this; but it certainly chimed, for what this is worth, with my own personal assessment of opinion based on two separate visits to the area, each of several days duration. Partly it was the David-and-Goliath syndrome; partly the flamboyant muck-and-brass Toryism of the industrial north; but there was also, I suspect, another force at work. The Tameside public, having recovered from its indignation at the old I.Q.-based eleven plus, was now more ready to accept a kind of selection relying on teachers' assessments. This allowed them to continue to support the grammar schools and to reject comprehensive education – or rather, since the people of Tameside had no direct experience of it, the *image* of comprehensive education purveyed by television and newspapers.

The Tameside poll was followed in October 1977 by an opinion poll conducted for *The Sunday Times* by MORI (Market and Opinion Research International).[15] This showed that 71 per cent of voters were in favour of keeping the remaining grammar schools. So were a staggering 58 per cent of Labour voters.

Psephological evidence[16] suggests that Labour's plans for comprehensive education helped it return to power in 1964. Much the same arguments were advanced in 1966 and possibly once again weighed heavily with the floating voter. But if the *Sunday Times* poll of 1977 was right, a very substantial shift of opinion had now occurred, and not in Tameside alone.

Just as the grammar school campaigners of the 1960s forgot what this meant for the secondary moderns, so today's retentionists ignore, or, more probably, are genuinely ignorant of, the disadvantages of coexistence. But even if these were more generally understood, it seems quite likely that many people would still want to keep the grammar schools. For there remains, as any casual observer of British society must acknowledge, a deep distrust of anything with even a tinge of egalitarianism about it.

This was demonstrated, almost comically, in the case of the direct grant schools. There were 172 of these basically fee-paying grammar schools. Each received a substantial government grant for keeping 25 per cent or more of its places open to pupils from the maintained (or 'state') system. Parents of these pupils enjoyed remittance of their fees on a sliding scale depending on their income. Though the schools were invited by Circular 10/65 to 'associate' themselves with comprehensive reform, only one or two did so. In 1966 the Secretary of State warned them that he would take action. In 1970 the second report of the Public Schools Commission said firmly that 'if maintained grammar schools are being reorganized ... it is indefensible ... to preserve and support other grammar schools having similar functions'. Finally, in 1974, Reg Prentice, as Labour Education Secretary, announced that the direct grant would be discontinued. And what did the direct grant schools do? Almost all of them went independent, so that, as a by-product of comprehensive reform, 119 private schools were set up at a stroke. The intensity of feeling on this issue has been shown by the schools' success in keeping going independently, despite intimidating fees.

Independent schools generally, and particularly the more famous public schools, have continued to do well throughout the period of comprehensive reform, taking some 6 per cent of our whole school population and almost by definition the children of the wealthiest. The mere existence of this sector is obviously the greatest threat of all, whatever the excellence of the individual schools, to the kind of social unity envisaged by the post-war reformers. As Shirley Williams said in an interview with *The Times Educational Supplement* in 1976:[17] 'The argument about independent schools is an argument about class. If people are educated separately, they are likely to remain separate. They will never mix and I don't think we can afford that.' This is different in an important way from the argument over 'creaming'. The grammar schools damage the comprehensives of the comprehensive system by taking out the top ability band. The independent schools, in general, select more by wealth than by ability, and so the damage is mainly social.

Ironically, however, in view of the clientele which the public schools serve, they enjoy charitable status, worth about 7 per cent of their annual outlay. The Ministry of Defence and the Foreign Office also pay almost £40 million a year to send to them the children of employees serving overseas.

To attack the public schools frontally, however, is something that no Labour Government has ever dared to do, no matter how deeply committed to the principle of equality of opportunity. This is partly because many of the products of the public schools occupy powerful positions in British society and remain committed to their educational origins. As a result, the rumpus would be enormous. Charges of 'levelling' would once again arise – and this time with a good deal more justification. For the public schools, though they take only 6 per cent of the school population, are responsible for 14 per cent of those taking 'A' levels, 20 per cent of all those in sixth forms and over 20 per cent of all successful applicants to university – and this, of course, on the basis of a student body selected by wealth rather than intellect.

But Labour's diffidence also owes something to respect for the principle of freedom of choice for parents (a matter which, as we shall see in a moment, is now becoming vitally important inside the maintained sector). The freedom to opt for private education is widely regarded as an inalienable right, whatever its consequences for everybody else, and it was in fact a Labour Government which in 1977 signed the United Nations Covenant on Economic, Social and Cultural rights. This acknowledged the right of parents to choose for their children 'schools other than those established by the public authorities'. British support for the principle seemed to rule permanently out of court any attempt to abolish the public schools.

Meanwhile, however, one or two limited moves to trim the public schools had been attempted. Labour's election manifesto of 1974 contained a pledge to withdraw the advantages of charitable status. In 1975 a House of Commons committee agreed that this should happen unless the public schools could show they met 'a range of clear educational needs throughout the whole community'. But not long afterwards, the committee set up to close the charity loophole announced, amazingly, that it had been unable to find a formula for doing so. The project was apparently abandoned.

A potentially more effective approach was opened up by the 1976 Education Act which obliged local education authorities to ask the Secretary of State's permission before taking up places in private education. At the time of its enactment, about 40,000 places in private schools were being taken up each year by local authorities. Some of these were justified by shortage of suitable places, particularly boarding school places, in maintained schools. But an inquiry by *The Times Educational Supplement* in 1977[18] revealed that most were in fact taken up by forty-six local authorities. These places accounted, on average, for 2·4 per cent of their secondary school population (in one case 10·9 per cent). Seven of what were now eight 'rebel' authorities and almost all of the twenty-six considered 'semi-rebels' were among the forty-six. Four-fifths of the forty-six authorities were Conservative and many of them were sending off their brightest children. This meant, of course, a continuing element of selection by ability even in supposedly all-through comprehensive areas. The Secretary of State's new powers gave her the opportunity to stop this and so, in one respect at least, to limit the damage done to the comprehensive sector by the public schools. Whether or not this was fair to the brightest children remained a matter of bitter controversy.

At the same time, the enthusiasm for selective education of all kinds – whether in grammar schools, the former direct grant schools, in public or other independent schools – encouraged Conservative planners to adopt a set of policies which were in their essentials deeply inimical to the comprehensive sector, whatever their likely effect on gifted children. Broadly, the plan was to preserve surviving grammar schools and to reintroduce selection by ability in a number of new ways.

The first aim, the preservation of the grammar schools, was to be achieved by repeal of the 1976 Education Act. Repeal would have the additional effect of making it easier once again for local authorities to take up places in private schools. Another element in the plan was the reintroduction of the direct grant schools in a new form. In a series of speeches and then in a policy pamphlet[19] in December 1977, Mr St John-Stevas promised to introduce a country-wide network of semi-independent schools offering 25 per cent or more of their places to children from the maintained sector. The schools themselves would select these children. (One of the features of the direct grant schools was that they were very poorly distributed, with almost none in Wales, for instance, and a disproportionate number in Cheshire and Lancashire.) For the parents there would be partial or total remission of fees 'in accordance with a generous income scale'. This would be funded centrally, not by local authorities. The whole programme, according to Mr St John-

Stevas, would cost about £50 million a year; and both in public and in private he was assiduous in fostering the impression that Mrs Thatcher, as Conservative leader, was deeply committed to the project. Some other influential Conservatives, however, put the cost higher and doubted the availability of treasury funds.

The other main way in which selection was to be re-introduced was by encouraging comprehensive schools to specialize in particular subjects. If over-subscribed, each of these schools would be allowed 'to select the pupils most likely to excel at its speciality'. This, Conservative spokesmen explained, could take place at any age from eleven to fourteen.

The extraordinary thing about this plan was that it was accompanied by a pledge, accepted at face value by most commentators, to make the comprehensives work. And only the feeblest attempt was made in the Conservative document to assert that coexistence need not damage the comprehensives – comprehensives and selective schools could 'coexist peacefully side by side' was the ambiguous phrase used.

This is a question of numbers. It is obvious that if a third, for example, of the available children are going to selective schools it is not possible to have comprehensive schools as well. But it is quite different if the percentage going to the selective schools is a lower one, say three or five per cent. In fact one can go up to ten per cent and still leave the comprehensive schools with a *reasonable* number of above average ability children.[20] (My italics.)

The statement was reinforced by figures from Bristol which purported to show that in a mixed system comprehensives could still have an *'adequate'* (my italics) top. Much depends on what is meant by 'reasonable' and 'adequate'.

The point to be made here is not that Mr St John-Stevas's plans lacked merit. They might have a good deal of merit if society wished to prefer its brightest children at the expense of the duller ones. The point is that by sleight of hand the Conservatives had been claiming that they supported comprehensive education while they were in fact manoeuvring towards the restoration of something closer to the old bipartite system.

In summary, then, it is clear that comprehensive reform is at present, and whether for better or for worse, fragile and incomplete. Conservative rejection of the fundamental premise of 'indivisibility' means that it is unlikely to be permanent. Public realization of this is generally obscured by lack of clarity in terminology.

One other important and highly perplexing matter still remains to be discussed before we can move on from the politics of comprehensive reorganization. This is the conflict within the comprehensive sector between neighbourhood schools and freedom of parental choice. For most people in Britain, apart from the 6 per cent with enough money to opt for private education, there is at present no real freedom of choice of secondary school. In rural areas there is generally only one school which a child can reasonably attend. In most cities, schools are either strictly zoned or 'fed' from certain specified primary schools. This means that, to the extent to which they are untouched by selection, the schools provide for all the pupils in their own area. One argument in favour of this arrangement is that it greatly improves the chances of community involvement; the school, in a real sense, belongs to its neighbourhood. Ideally, it will exercise a socially unifying influence. One notable drawback, however, is that where an area is depressed – classically in the inner city – a neighbourhood school may be composed almost entirely of children who are already at a disadvantage. Many Conservatives argue that grammar schools provide the best hope of escape for able, inner-city children. Although this argument has been pressed with great conviction, it unfortunately ignores the great mass of children of average ability. The alternative advocated by comprehensive supporters is the concentration of extra resources on these schools.

One additional possibility is to distribute children of comparable ability evenly through the system, so that each school gets a representative proportion of bright, average and less-bright children. Obviously this cannot be done over too great a distance – because of the difficulty of travelling – and for this reason it is only a partial solution to the problem of 'social mix'.

But at least it means that each school has the challenge of providing for its share of the able – a stimulus eagerly welcomed by most schools and likely to prevent the appearance of out and out 'sink' schools. This system is known as banding,[21] and it is operated, along with limited parental choice, in London and one or two other areas. Though it involves an element of selection by ability, it does not mean, of course, that brighter children are selected *out* of the system and so it was permitted, subject to the Secretary of State's discretion, in the 1976 Education Act.

Zoning is obviously irreconcilable with parental choice. Banding implies clear limitations to it. Only about a third of local authority areas try to offer anything approaching unlimited parental choice and they can attempt to do so only because most people in practice choose the nearest school. The difficulty in offering choice is that popular schools become oversubscribed in districts where there is a large child population. When this happens, priority is normally given to those who live nearest or already have brothers and sisters in the school. Inevitably some are disappointed, and their disappointment is all the more bitter where parents have succumbed to the illusion that they could exercise total freedom in the choice of a limited commodity. Most families bite the bullet and accept what they are given. But hundreds every year refuse to send their children to schools they consider unsatisfactory. Groups often band together to provide some kind of interim education and the state of the law is such that, in the end, if they hold their children out long enough, and are prepared to go through all the stages of appeal, they can generally get them into the school of their first choice. Legislation to change this – by allowing a local authority to declare a school full up – was under consideration in 1977 but was shelved, partly through lack of parliamentary time and partly because the egalitarian wing of the Labour party believes that choice of *any* kind destroys the principle of neighbourhood schools and were not prepared to countenance this.

The combined effect of choice and the present appeal system is clearly damaging to schools and to the children in them. In

December 1977, in a paper drawn up for a top-level conference on comprehensive education, specially convened by the Secretary of State as part of the follow-up to the 'Great Debate', Manchester's chief education officer, Dudley Fiske, declared in round terms that the operation of choice had seriously distorted the city's schools. Some schools were heavily over-subscribed while others had up to 800 empty places. There was, he said, a 'hierarchy of popularity', based on tradition, fashion and prejudice. Children with above average non-verbal intelligence quotient were concentrated in some schools; children with lower scores were concentrated in others. The great number of feeder schools contributing to some individual secondary schools caused difficulties in the curriculum. Parents who were less aspirant, less articulate or less competent in handling an appeal, allowed their children to attend less popular schools. 'Whatever else it might be called, the result is certainly not a system of broadly similar comprehensive schools. Some argue it is not a comprehensive system at all', said Mr Fiske, concluding that perhaps the time had come to think and talk more of the needs of children than of the rights of parents.

The difficulty, however, is that both leading politicians and the most articulate members of the public believe the right of choice to be a fundamental liberty. As with the public schools, there is a simple conflict between the principles of individual freedom and anything approaching equality of opportunity. Politically, the area is a minefield.

While left-wingers believe in the neighbourhood school and would be prepared to see parental choice diminished, middle-of-the-road Labour politicians are well aware of the political advantages of offering choice, talk about it a great deal, but have not yet devised any formula for offering it without creating a 'Manchester-type effect' throughout the country. The best they seem likely to manage is to guarantee a right of choice by religious denomination or according to preference for co-education or single-sex schooling. This is theoretically built into the 1944 Act but is at the moment meaningless, without resort to appeal, in the many areas where schools are strictly zoned.

The Conservatives welcome choice openly, believing it to be the most powerful sanction against inadequate schools. Their stance on this issue is related to the enthusiasm which some of them have shown in recent years for experimenting with the education voucher. Under the kind of scheme discussed during the years of Conservative opposition from 1970, parents in areas chosen for experiment would receive an annual voucher representing the average cost of a year's state schooling for each child. They would take this voucher along to the school of their choice (themselves paying any extra if the school was an independent one). The number of pupils who chose the school would thus determine the level of its income. Popular schools would flourish and, at the most extreme, unsatisfactory schools would presumably have to close.[22] Today, however, it is clear that because of a sharply falling school population – it is expected to drop from about 8,980,000 in 1977 to 7,480,000 in 1986 – a great many schools will have to close in any case. By giving free choice to parents, allowing them to patronize popular schools and avoid the unpopular, many of the effects of the voucher could be obtained without its use. As Martin Lightfoot, a former senior education officer in Inner London, wrote in *The Times Educational Supplement*,[23]

Where there is slack in the system, and where parents are allowed an almost totally free choice within that system, some schools will close themselves because nobody wants to go there. The result will be an increasingly intense competition between schools for a dwindling number of children.

This kind of competition between schools, with some developing strongly, perhaps with beneficial results in academic standards, and others dwindling painfully towards death, seems to be the inevitable consequence of present Conservative policies. Labour politicians and most educational administrators, while offering no very clear solution to the problem of the unpopular school, believe that the exercise of unlimited choice at a time of falling rolls would bring almost unlimited chaos. This is why Labour's failure to legislate, or even to issue a circular, in 1977 to allow authorities to state the operating capacity of individual schools may turn out to have been a critical omission.

Notes

1. *Education in Schools, A Consultative Document* (H.M.S.O., Cmd 6869).
2. Fenwick, I. G. K., *The Comprehensive School, 1944–1970* (Methuen, 1976).
3. Crossman, R. H. S. (ed.), *New Fabian Essays* (Turnstile Press, 1952).
4. Bulletin No. 35, Department of the Interior, Bureau of Education (1918).
5. *Children and Their Primary Schools* (H.M.S.O., 1967).
6. Yates, Alfred, and Pidgeon, D. A., *Admission to Grammar School* (Newnes (for N.F.E.R.), 1957).
7. Douglas, J. W. B., *The Home and the School* (MacGibbon and Kee, 1964).
8. Benn, Caroline, and Simon, Brian, *Half Way There* (McGraw-Hill, 1970, Penguin, 1972).
9. Labour Party Annual Conference, 1963.
10. See *The Growth of Comprehensive Education*, D.E.S. Report on Education No. 87 (March 1977).
11. Cox, C. B., and Dyson, A. E. (ed.), *Fight for Education, a Black Paper* (Critical Quarterly Society, 1969).
12. Quoted by Kogan, Maurice, *Educational Policy Making* (George Allen and Unwin Ltd, 1975).
13. *Comprehensive Education – our last chance?* (Campaign for Comprehensive Education and the Programme for Reform in Secondary Education, December 1977).
14. Benn, Caroline, and Simon, Brian, *Half Way There*, Penguin edition of 1972, p. 425 *et seq.*
15. 2 October 1977.
16. Fenwick, I. G. K., *The Comprehensive School, 1944–1970* (Methuen, 1976), p. 129.
17. 19 November 1976.
18. 18 February 1977.
19. St John-Stevas MP, Norman, *Better Schools for All* (Conservative Political Centre, 1977).

20. St John-Stevas MP, Norman, *Better Schools for All* (Conservative Political Centre, 1977).
21. 'Banding' can also mean the division of children into broad ability bands *within* a school. This practice is discussed below, p. 65 *et seq.*
22. Two incidental but important points should also be made about the voucher system. Firstly, it would not, in practice, solve the problem of choice. Popular schools would fill up, and late comers would have to be directed elsewhere. Secondly, the system is intended by its adherents to include private as well as maintained schools. It would thus be a means of subsidy to the private sector.
23. 8 July 1977.

2. Developments inside school

The growth of the comprehensives over the past two and a half decades has been accompanied by a brisk evolution in the aims, method and content of teaching throughout the system. These changes began in infant teaching (so far as public education was concerned), moved on into junior schools and are now reaching right up into the sixth form, though at this level affecting mainly those young people less likely to go on to higher education. From time to time the new approach has caused open anxiety. Primary school parents in the late 1940s, for instance, were worried about 'activity methods'. But most energy has been taken up for most of the time, as described in the last chapter, by arguments over the grammar schools. It was only in 1969, with the publication of the first Black Paper, that worry over method began to be expressed at all systematically. That worry continued to grow during the 1970s, and the gathering stream became a flood with the start of Mr Callaghan's Great Debate. All the passion that had gone into the comprehensive argument seemed now to be diverted into a critique of modern practice. Much of the rest of this book will be taken up with a discussion of what is wrong, or said to be wrong, inside our schools and what, if anything, is likely to be done about it. But first it seems necessary to establish a little more firmly what is meant by a modern approach and the extent to which it is applied. That is the main purpose of this chapter.

The difficulty is that any description which seems at all favourable will be taken by opponents of modern practice as pre-empting fair evaluation of their case; and vice versa with supporters of the modern. In these trying circumstances it seems best to concentrate quite openly on schools which enjoy good reputations in their areas. I have chosen one informal primary school, one purpose-built comprehensive where teaching methods in some departments are highly informal and, by way of contrast, one rather more traditional comprehensive. By looking at what they do, I hope that the reader will be able to form some impression of what is intended by good practitioners, whether ancient, modern or in between, and some idea of the problems they encounter. This may help to put later arguments into perspective. First, though, a word about the theory behind the practice.

Most public education in most countries was based until about the time of the First World War on the belief that the main function of school was to drill children in reading, writing and arithmetic and to induce them to memorize a good deal of fact, sometimes useful, sometimes, in retrospect, bizarre. I have on my desk a book called *The Child's Guide to Knowledge*, fifty-fifth edition, dated 1884, from which my brother's godmother's mother was taught at a school in the industrial north. This includes such exchanges as:

Q. Where were blankets first made?
A. At Bristol; they are so named from Thomas Blanket, who, in 1340, first set up the looms there for weaving these comfortable articles.

or this:

Q. How high is the Asiatic elephant?
A. Usually from nine to ten feet, with ears of a moderate size; the African rarely exceeds eight feet, having remarkably long ears spreading over the shoulders, and its countenance exhibits the same inferiority.

or this (the book gives me such pleasure I find it hard to stop):

Q. What English king wore the first pair of knit silk stockings?
A. Henry II. The invention of them came from Spain; but they were not heard of again till the reign of Henry VIII and Edward VI.

The system rested on good order, discipline and repetition. It was, at best, efficient; at worst, it was brutal and repressive. There was a minimum of distraction. Janetta Bowie, in an entertaining volume of autobiography about teaching on Clydeside of the 1930s[1] recals how, as a probationer, she stood alone in front of fifty first-year infants, equipped only with blackboard and a piece of chalk. (One of her fellow teachers remembered classes of 150.) But by 1930, writes Miss Bowie, with a decided twinkle, there was already a theory creeping into Clydeside that children should be 'encouraged to develop in their own way'. This theory, for all practical purposes, had had its origin during the Italian Renaissance when Vittorino da Feltre asserted that one of the main facts about children was their difference from one another. These differences, he said, should be respected; it was the teacher's job to make their education enjoyable. John Milton echoed this. To be effective, he wrote, learning should be 'easy and delightful'. Even the most intractable material could be made to seem enjoyable when properly approached. Comenius, the great seventeenth-century Czech teacher and preacher, believed that, just as artisans learned to forge by forging, so children should learn to write by writing. Instead of a diet of books and nothing else, children should learn 'from the living book of the world', and their learning, rather than being a mass of unrelated facts, should make clear sense to them. Rousseau, perhaps the most important of all in philosophical terms, wrote in *Émile* in 1762 that each individual should learn by making his own discoveries and he described what he thought to be the natural, and immutable, progression in the mental development of the child. Friedrich Froebel, in 1826, said that play was the foundation of learning and that the purpose of education was to develop the natural gifts of the child. In our own century, John Dewey, the American philosopher, has been highly influential in winning supporters for this kind of thinking.

The precursors of today's 'modern' approach are almost innumerable. What most have had in common is a belief in the individuality and individual worth of the child; the belief that a teacher should try to bring those virtues out, rather than impose unquestioning obedience to a code; belief that fact should be a tool for understanding rather than something learned parrot-wise; belief that play should be a means of learning; and, above all, a belief that learning should be a happy experience.

Some of these ideas were applied quite early on in public education in an episodic, experimental manner. They began to enter the mainstream of public education in America and Britain during the 1920s and 1930s, receiving at that time a considerable boost from behaviourist psychologists who showed that pleasurable reward was a better stimulant than punishment to 'operant conditioning' – the process by which problem-solving behaviour is reinforced. Jean Piaget, an extremely influential Swiss psychologist who was at the peak of his activity during the 1950s, mapped out the growth of the child's mind in a way that strongly reinforced the belief in 'learning by doing' both for young children and for some older ones as well – by the use of real objects in addition and subtraction, for example, rather than by numerical calculation alone.

There were, thought Piaget, certain well-defined stages which every child went through, had to go through, to grow. These always occurred in the same order, cumulatively, with one stage preparing the way for the next. And the child, Piaget implied, could not be hurried along unduly from one stage to the next. In the first three of the four stages – that is to say, up to the age of about eleven – the child in his mental processes relied heavily on his experience of physical reality. Only in the fourth stage, the teenage years, could he begin to handle abstract concepts easily.

In the introduction to a symposium on his work, Piaget wrote:[2]

It is absolutely necessary that learners have at their disposal concrete material experiences (and not merely pictures), and that they form their own hypotheses and verify them (or not verify them) themselves through their active manipulations. The observed activities, including those of the teacher, are not formative of new organizations in the child.

To a growing number of teachers, the modernist prospectus seemed both humane and eminently practical; and they began to look for ways of applying these ideals. The beginning came in infant school because there was less in the way of formal curriculum and play was more readily accepted there as a medium of learning. (The idea of the importance of play is not, to be honest, entirely easy to those who have grown up in a formal environment. It came as a shock to me when, as a lecturer in a polytechnic, I realized that perhaps the most eye-opening activity in the whole of a year's course had been a role-playing 'game' during which students had had either to make out a case for receiving a council house or else to allocate council housing to some but not to others.)

Junior schools remained formal longer than infant schools, largely because of the eleven-plus and the race for grammar school. But as the eleven-plus began to disappear, a more 'modern' approach crept up through the age range. In almost all parts of the country there is now much greater emphasis on the happiness of the child, the cheerfulness of the environment and, of course, a greater range of equipment available than in Janetta Bowie's days as a probationer – everything from poster paint to measuring rods and possibly tape recorders. Much light and bright equipment was in evidence when Miss Bowie and I made a joint tour of Clydeside schools in 1975 to see how times had changed.

But in some areas, the process of change has gone a good deal further.

Prior Weston, a combined infant and junior school in the City of London, is a good example. I was drawn to the school by the publication of a book by the head teacher[3] which asserted many of the principles of a modern type of education at a time when they were already coming under attack. Children were individuals, wrote Henry Pluckrose, but 'the embryo of all that is real in learning' lay in qualities which children shared – the wish to play and talk, their delight in movement, their curiosity and imagination. And then he added three more characteristics which may surprise those whose notion of modern schooling is derived from hostile accounts. These were: a child's sense of responsibility, his traditionalism, and his need for security. By the development of the more outgoing characteristics, in a secure society where child and adult freely interacted, children could make the most of all their abilities, wrote Pluckrose. The aim of the 'open school' was to be that secure society.

Now it is often the case that head teachers who are long on theory are a little short on execution. But I decided, just in case, to pay a visit to the school. In the event, I stayed for a week and immediately afterwards wrote these notes. Later comments are in square brackets.

Prior Weston School

Prior Weston School occupies a modern, single-storey building in London EC1. Two-thirds of its children are traditional East Enders; one-third are from middle-class homes. [This is highly untypical of the inner city. In terms of intake, the appropriate comparison is with a wealthy suburban area.]

The telephone is out of order so I drop by and ask for Henry Pluckrose, author and head teacher. I find him on his knees among a cluster of children. He says all visitors are welcome. [So, I learn later, is publicity. In this the school differs sharply from many others which are equally successful. It turns out that one of the school's main tactics, for pedagogical, as well as other, purposes, is the unabashed exploitation of any passing adult.]

When I return for my full week at school, the first thing I notice is the quietness – helped along, admittedly, by carpets in many parts of the building. There is a lot of talk but the voices are calm. There is also frequent movement as groups of children rearrange themselves for some fresh topic or activity. But there is little wild running and little silliness. Everybody is quietly getting on. The other thing I notice is the vividness of the paintings and other artifacts which cover the walls in a rotating display of work in progress.

Against this background, I make a note of what is missing. There appear to be no syllabus, no timetable, no formal division of work into school subjects, no specific playtimes. There are no separate classes or classrooms. There is not even a staffroom. My week is devoted to working out the invisible structures that underlie the day at Prior Weston.

Organization

Prior Weston is divided into an upper and a lower school, the break occurring at nine, not at the usual age of eight. Children aged from five to eight inclusive are grouped together in 'families' of about twenty. They have a home base in a particular area and a teacher who is concerned mainly with that home base. From it, the children range out in small groups to take part in activities in other bases. On Monday, for example, children from one area may be reading and writing 'at home', while groups go off to another base for painting or work with numbers. Children are dealt with individually, joining whichever group is thought appropriate.

In the upper school, nine-year-olds form a single group and spend a year of consolidation. The ten- and eleven-year-olds are again grouped together and work in the same way as in the lower school. The difference, Pluckrose says, is a longer concentration span. 'When they begin an activity more is expected of them.'

There are 215 children in the school, rising to 250 in summer. Pluckrose says in his book that 320 is the largest number suitable for this kind of school.

Learning

The only specific aims are that the children should learn to read and write, be numerate and socially adjusted. Pluckrose says: 'Young people are failing society because they have no social grace.' He defines this as a sense of cooperation and responsibility.

I join the nine-year-olds to see what happens in practice. Rikki Hutchings, their teacher, is the daughter of a barber, a graduate, married and expecting a baby in three months. She has the gift, shared by many experienced primary teachers, of winning silence when she wants it by sitting up straight and waiting. Usually she is on her feet, moving from table to table in a gently buzzing concourse. She calls the children 'darling' with the comfortable even-handedness of a bus conductress.

The first activity, to my surprise, is entirely formal. The children are doing joined-up handwriting, copying long lines of letters in books which contain examples prepared individually by Rikki. Nine-year-old Emma says to me: 'I hate it. It makes my arm tired.' Most seem to enjoy the simple, repetitive activity. Rikki says traditional teaching methods are used wherever they seem likely to be more effective.

The main task of the day is preparation for a trip to the Tower of London. The Tower is nearby and the children go there quite frequently. They make about four local excursions each term. The history, geography and society of the neighbourhood are among their main studies. For Rikki today the problem is how to make the Tower fresh and useful. She duplicates a set of sketch maps and the children fill in the names of various buildings. Our visit seems to be turning into an exercise in mapping and map-reading. We also discuss the history of the Tower and decide to make drawings of various objects among the Crown Jewels.

Next day, on the underground, the children behave impeccably. At the Tower, map-reading and sketching proceed pleasantly but purposefully. It all seems fairly normal for a well-planned outing – until one of the Beefeaters begins to talk to us.

At that moment, without warning and to the visible surprise of the Beefeater, all the children fling themselves full-length on the ground, some to draw pictures of him, others to take notes. The impulse to observe and record has been brought out in these children to an extraordinary degree.

I also note what I take to be the growth of understanding.

The slowest girl in the group has attached herself to me. We find a dead pigeon under an arrow-slit. 'Look,' she says, 'it got killed in the war.' She thinks a moment. 'No, no,' she cries, 'it's got an arrer in it.'

Back at school in the afternoon, the nine-year-olds begin to produce guide-books to the Tower, made up of paintings, drawings and their own writing. This will take about two days and will not be abandoned until it is finished. 'Completion is very important', says Rikki. Pluckrose says: 'You go from a positive experience on the child's part to a deeper understanding.'

All day Rikki has been talking to the children, putting things one way, then another, continually trying to expand their use of language.

I mention that our day seems highly structured. Rikki comments: 'Some people think modern teaching methods mean the teacher shouldn't lead and should just let them do their own thing. But it doesn't work. Student teachers go into a class and say, "Right, then, kids, what do you want to do?" and they get chaos right away. The state where children make their own decisions represents a very high point of discipline. You must first be in total control. Children can only know what they want from a tight, secure structure.' [The question of whether or not most teachers can achieve this in an informal setting – and, more important, how many of them in fact intend to – is central to the debate and I shall return to it later. The issues are political and philosophical as well as educational.]

Another main theme is mutual cooperation. At present work is in progress on an extension to the building and in the lower school many children are keeping individual diaries of progress. I spend an afternoon among six-year-olds who, as they write their diaries, continually exchange words and spellings. If they get stuck, they ask the nearest adult.

During my week at Prior Weston the architect in charge of the extension (who was also the designer of the main school) spends most of an afternoon with the older children. An actress comes to give a talk, fresh trainee teachers are welcomed and set to work. All adults spend a lot of time answering questions.

Standards

In the lower school, maths is taught by the usual modern methods. These include sorting objects into sets, counting and measuring them, and so forth. In the upper school there is a mixture of formal work on topics – volume, say, or area – and individual work designed to illuminate the nature and relationship of numbers. Some children achieve a very high standard. [I am surprised, looking back, at my readiness to pass judgement, even though this seemed commonsensical at the time. The question of how to evaluate achievement is, of course, highly contentious and is dealt with at some length in Chapter Four.]

Reading and writing are taught by a combination of many methods. I have heard of parents unhappy with results, but Pluckrose claims a high success rate. Of this year's thirty-six nine-year-olds, for instance, all are reading. Five are marginally below normal reading age, only three are poor readers. Informal testing bears this out.

Writing is vivid and sensitive but often full of spelling mistakes. 'That doesn't matter so much,' says Pluckrose. 'Above all else I want them to use the courageous word.' But I notice that the mistakes are often in the simplest words.

Behind the apparent fluidity of the timetable there is in fact a detailed system of record-keeping so that it is usually possible to say what point each child has reached in each main subject area. This is clearly essential to the Prior Weston method.

Teachers

There are nine teachers, including Pluckrose. They spend almost all day with the children. But after lunch they sit together in the library area. These meetings are quiet and low key, concerned mainly with the organization of the next twenty-four hours. It is through them that the school's unity of purpose is continuously defined and modified.

As well as giving up their lunch hour, the teachers are expected to arrive early or stay late. While they are at work, they

are continuously visible to one another. 'It's hard to slack', one
of the younger teachers tells me. As a group they appear to have
the kind of talents and limitations one might expect in any staff
room. What distinguishes them is common purpose and willing-
ness to cooperate.

Discipline

A child who behaves badly gets ticked off – 'and not half', says
Pluckrose. 'If a child is to grow he must be challenged by an
adult he respects when his behaviour is unacceptable. But to hit
a child is an admission of defeat.'

Respect

Each day there is an assembly of the whole school. A chosen
theme is illustrated by a particular group usually with music,
acting and reading aloud, both from books and the children's
own work. Assembly is popular. But many of the smaller per-
formers are inaudible. 'We hope they will be audible by the age
of eight,' says Pluckrose. But isn't it boring for the rest? 'Not at
all,' says Pluckrose, 'that's how they show respect for the five-
year-olds.'

At lunch the older children serve the younger ones. This generally works well but the only loutish behaviour I observe all
week comes from a 'server' who is careless and rude – to me
and everybody at his table.

Music

One of the teachers is occupied full-time with music, and supported by violin and 'cello instructors. There is musical activity
throughout the day with elaborate part-song and orchestral
playing. Margo Fagan, the music teacher, says: 'For orchestral
work, self-discipline is what you need.'

Community

Pluckrose tries to work within the expectations of parents and community, nudging people along the Prior Weston path but not insisting. 'In the long term, we cannot change the content and style of the school day to any marked degree without parental support', Pluckrose wrote in his book. If possible, contact is established early with mothers of pre-school children. They are invited to visit whenever they want. More and more relationships are being established with the adult world and a certain amount of social casework is carried out from the school. Once a month the head teacher and representatives of the main support agencies – education welfare officer, psychiatric social worker, educational psychologist – meet and consider difficult cases, frequently with the parents.

During my week at Prior Weston one child got into trouble outside school. His disturbance was first noticed by a voluntary adult helper; at the daily meeting the teachers were briefed to be on the alert; the father was contacted that same afternoon. Next morning the father came to school; the (serious) issue was brought into the open and the child made to realize how close he had come to getting himself into a desperate situation. No angry words were spoken.

Facts, feelings

Pluckrose is discussing passion and revenge with a group from the upper school. He illustrates his points with readings from poets of the First World War. It is strong stuff. The children listen attentively, argue, develop themes. They know about Northern Ireland, the Arab–Israeli conflict, the Christian–Muslim conflict in Beirut. 'People should stay their own religion and that's that', says one boy. Another thinks religious war is 'just a waste of people'. Afterwards Pluckrose says: 'Modern teachers are being crucified because they don't teach facts, facts, facts. But modern children have a lot of facts and it's the interpretation of facts and feelings that makes them civilised.'

In retrospect, it is clear that Prior Weston enjoys various advantages over many other schools – among them a willing and receptive clientele without conspicuous learning problems, and a new building which promotes the kind of circulation the school aims for. It might be a different matter if there were 500 pupils, many from overseas, in an old three-decker of the kind that looms so often in the middle of our industrial cities. But two general points which could equally well apply to any other primary school stand out. The first is that the apparent spontaneity is based on hard work. Teachers can take advantage of opportunities as they arise because they know where they are with what they are doing and have a clear idea of their aims. This is related to the second point. Despite the outward ease, and though it proceeds by enlisting the cooperation of the children, Prior Weston is very much under adult control. Some might say that this was a conservative approach.

At the same time, the school relies on almost all the teaching tactics which are generally considered characteristic of a progressive, child-centred method. Some of these are: 'individualized work'; topic work; 'family' or 'vertical' grouping of children of different ages; 'learning by doing'; abandonment of a formal timetable in favour of the 'integrated day' in which a subject of interest can be pursued without constraint or several different activities can be going on at once. There is also a much less hierarchical relationship between staff and children than in a formal school.

Looking at informal education on a national basis, however, what seems most striking of all is the patchy way in which the approach is being applied. The Plowden Report of 1967, which came down foursquare in favour of progressive methods and was accordingly a key document in making them acceptable, said the progressive movement was a 'general and quickening trend' and implied that about a third of primary schools were substantially affected by change in outlook and method. But various, more recent research papers have established that even today the proportion is smaller than this – in the case of Lancashire only 17 per cent.[4] 'Many remain firmly traditional while the majority aim at a compromise with a traditional bias', wrote Nigel Wright in 1977 after a careful review of the evidence.[5]

In practice, this seems to mean that many schools wear an outwardly informal air, with plenty of individual and topic work and islands of desks instead of old-fashioned rows. But there is also, as Virginia Makins found when she spent time in ten junior schools for *The Times Educational Supplement*,[6] a good deal of teaching that would be familiar to the older generation – timetables, columns of sums, drills in grammar, punctuation and comprehension. She was critical of elements in both approaches; but her major impressions confirmed my own, accumulated over several years of school visiting: 'junior schools these days are happy places'. It is almost always a pleasure to go into one.

The same statement cannot be made with equal confidence of secondary schools. A visitor tends to come away with far more complicated reactions. Some secondary schools are cheerful and outwardly pleasing; in others, bare walls and empty faces confront the visitor. More generally, as might be expected with institutions so much larger – and inhabited to a large extent by adolescents – one can observe both alienation and eager participation under the same roof (or, as is often the case, under several roofs up to a mile apart). Whether matters are getting worse or better is clearly a major public issue. But the approach has certainly been changing in many important ways.

Many changes spring ultimately from the same liberal philosophy that informs the more progressive junior schools – ideas about the worth of the individual, for instance – but rather than adding up to a general approach they have more often occurred as specific responses to specific needs. The overwhelmingly important example of this has been in the development of exams.

Inescapably the old grammar schools were dominated by exams. These were set by the university examining boards and they reflected the approach and ideals of the universities. Knowledge of many facts was the main prerequisite of success. In the case of older pupils, there was also considerable respect for ability in argument and sometimes for intellectual elegance. During the years between the two world wars the main exams were the School Certificate and Higher School Certificate, and to pass either of them a candidate had to take a group of subjects simultaneously as proof of a sound general education. The modern G.C.E. exam – the so-called General Certificate of Education with 'O' levels at sixteen and 'A' levels at eighteen – arrived in 1951; but though it still enshrined many of the university ideals, there had been one major change – subjects were now taken individually and certificates awarded for individual subjects. This both diminished university control of the curriculum and immediately gave much greater freedom of choice to school and pupil. Some believe that this is where the rot set in; others that it was the first real sign of adaptation to the modern world. In either event, it was only a beginning.

G.C.E. 'O' level was intended only for the most-able 20 per cent or so of the school population. At first, in a liberal-minded attempt to prevent the development of false academicism, secondary modern schools were forbidden to enter pupils for public exams. As evidence accumulated that many secondary-modern pupils were just as able as those in grammar schools, having been wrongly allocated at eleven-plus, this began to look absurd and the restriction was lifted. But that still left about 70 per cent of the school population, and their parents and prospective employers, clamouring for some kind of qualification in an increasingly qualification-hungry age. The growth of comprehensive schools, with the need to offer everybody something that could be presented as real opportunity, made the matter more urgent. Few realized that to increase the range of qualifications available would simply reinforce the schools as the central mechanism in sorting out which people would occupy which jobs in adult life. (Professor Ronald Dore of Sussex University has expounded this effect with great lucidity in his book *The Diploma Disease*.[7]) At the time, the benign response appeared to lie in the creation of a whole new range of certificates for the less-able. And so, in 1965, the C.S.E. – or Certificate of Secondary Education – was born.

A great deal of idealism went into C.S.E. Because the pupils taking it would not in general be aiming for higher education, it did not have to be at all the same as G.C.E. The cardinal difference was this: whereas the G.C.E. course led towards an exam which was the main point of the enterprise, C.S.E. could be framed as an assessment of the course the student had actually done, a servant of the classroom process and not its master. Teachers, not the universities, would devise the course according to what they saw as the needs of the students; and teachers were to be in control of the new, C.S.E. exam boards. The certificates themselves were to be awarded partly on the basis of exam performance but also on a continuous assessment of work during the two-year course. This was important since it implied that day-to-day work was of real value in itself.

Another important aspect of C.S.E. is that it comes (since 1970) in three forms, or 'modes'. Mode I is an externally marked exam, set by the new boards; Mode II is an externally marked exam set directly by teachers, usually for groups of schools; in Mode III, controversially, syllabus, assessment and marking are all in the hands of teachers in individual schools, and the only control is by external moderation, either statistical or in the form of visits from the C.S.E. boards. In theory, the top grade of C.S.E. (grade I) corresponds with a C grade in G.C.E. (this used to be the lowest passing grade before a reform which abolished pass and fail in favour of a series of grades descending well below the old pass mark). In practice, it is probably rather harder to get a C.S.E. grade I than a G.C.E. grade C; but much controversy, as we shall see, surrounds the lower grades in C.S.E. The whole new system also represents a formidable accretion of power into the hands of the teachers. The merits of this are a matter of bitter argument; but it should be noted that even some G.C.E. boards have begun to offer a Mode III option. At the same time, the C.S.E. approach has both coincided with and perhaps accelerated a range of intellectual developments affecting schools, universities, G.C.E. boards and even industry. These are generally less controversial than C.S.E. itself, but their effects are even more profound and have contributed a great deal to the uneasy sense that the old certainties of school are vanishing. I should like to illustrate the point by examining development in geography, a subject chosen because it is generally uncontroversial, and certainly not central enough to be the source of major argument in the way that English and mathematics are.

Along with *The Child's Guide to Knowledge*, I have on my desk as I write two books which make my case more eloquently than I can. The first is a perfectly respectable and conventional primer – *Britain and Overseas* by R. C. Honeybone and M. G. Goss, first published by Heinemann Educational Books in 1956 and reprinted six times in the first eight years of its life. The scrawled names in my copy – borrowed from a nearby secondary school – show that it was in use at least until 1972; and a quick flip through the text suggests that it is full of detailed and not altogether dull material. But it is the endpapers which reveal its inner nature. These contain a map of the world showing 'places visited in the book'. Outside Britain, the places are: an American cotton plantation, an Argentinian estancia, a Norwegian fiord [*sic*], a Saharan oasis, Nigerian village and so on. The chapter on the cotton plantation includes a picture of a mechanical cotton picker unloading into a wagon. 'Describe how the cotton picker is unloaded', exercise 14 enjoins.

The basic aim of this book is to provide the pupil with a solid layer of fact about places chosen, in general, for their uniqueness.

The other book is volume two of the *Oxford Geography Project*, first published by Oxford University Press in 1974. It is a very different matter. For a start, it is more attractive, the photographs livelier, the diagrams easier to follow. But, even more important, it is a book about ideas. Here, working away under an extended and interesting discussion of land use in Europe, one may recognize many of the major theories by which modern geographers have tried to explain the interaction between man and the world – Von Thunen's idea that land use becomes less intense as you move away from a centre of settlement; Burgess's pattern of concentric rings as a description of the growth of cities; Homer Hoyts notion that cities grow in segments along the lines of communication. Putting these ideas together, even in simple form, the twelve-year-old for whom the book is intended will get a lively idea of how things happen where they do. The same ideas, though in extended and more complex form, will still be under discussion and analysis at sixth-form level. Today, in the schools to which these ideas have percolated – probably a minority – the beginner begins with considerations of real value.

'Once you have done agriculture and the location of industry, you are made', said the young teacher who lent me the books. 'The rest follows, doesn't it? We are pushing principle all the time. Instead of going for uniqueness, we are looking at general patterns, trying to give the child the equipment to be able to explain anything he sees. If you've got the principles, then the facts about the region are easier to take in. But of course we do some good old-fashioned map-bashing as well. It's not much use if a child doesn't know where Spain is.'

This radical change of emphasis – from collection of fact to explanation – has come about because the study of geography has itself changed, turning in the last fifteen years or so from descriptive analysis to the study of processes in man and nature and in both together. In physical geography – basically the study of the Earth and the non-human factors operating on it – there has been a switch from interest in unravelling the past (the Ice Age and all that) to greater concentration on what is happening *now*. Human geography – the study of the way man affects his environment and it him – is now looked at not just in terms of man and nature but also in terms of economics (Californian farmers can afford to irrigate in their Mediterranean-type climate; warm, wet winters and hot, dry summers are of less relevance to them); of technology (look what the private car is doing to us and the way steel-making is moving to the coast); of people's perception of environment (will the decision on factory siting depend on the managing director's wife's impressions of the North of England even though she has never been there?); and so on through a mighty range of factors affecting human settlement, patterns of land use, the movement of goods and people[8]. Theoretical models are used to show the way things tend to work, and are abandoned where they prove less than useful. A lot of this can be described in statistical terms. Many of the processes can be made clear by simulation games. A favourite used to involve finding a site for a new London airport.

This new approach is now followed extensively in university departments and in 'A' level work in some sixth forms. As far as human geography goes, it has also made an impact on teaching lower down in comprehensives. The interpretative path is now sometimes followed by all pupils in the first two or three years of secondary schooling, and for those showing less academic ability there are excellent fourth- and fifth-year C.S.E. courses such as Geography for the Young School Leaver, devised at Avery Hill College in London but providing plenty of ideas and examples which teachers can adapt to the neighbourhood of their own schools. G.C.E. 'O' level has so far proved a little less flexible than C.S.E. or 'A' level and it is still easy to find such questions as: 'With the aid of annotated sketch maps, describe the position and importance of *two* of the following: Edinburgh; Leeds; Manchester; Plymouth; Southampton.' This is based on the old principle of the exhaustive study of regions and involves mainly the memorizing of fact.

In general, though, the study of geography – and no doubt 'O' level will soon catch up – relies rather more than it used to on the belief that true understanding depends upon understanding the relationship between facts and knowing how to find out facts when necessary rather than simply accumulating them. The partial adoption of this approach in geography is paralleled – episodically – in many other subjects. Some C.S.E. courses are openly dependent on it; more and more G.C.E. exams at 'A' level and 'O' level are changing in their nature because of it. But the interpretative approach depends essentially on a concept of culture which, though it accommodates itself easily to a liberal outlook, has not in fact been devised by liberals in the schools or even by the schools themselves. The schools are simply reflecting a shift of intellectual stance in society generally.

To return, though, to the actual operation of school. Apart from exams and the growth of the interpretative approach, the other main change has been in attitudes to 'streaming'. In the days of selection by ability it seemed entirely logical to grade individual classes according to ability. This carried over into some comprehensives so that, if there was an entry big enough to fill six forms (known in the trade as 'a six-form entry'), the pupils in those forms would be selected, so far as possible, in descending order of ability. This is called 'fine streaming'. Theoretically, it enables teachers to teach the whole class as one and to hit about the right intellectual level for everybody. But there turned out to be several important things wrong with this arrangement. If it had been hard to get the right children into the right schools under the eleven-plus, it was even harder to get them into the right streams. Much injustice was done. Streaming also tended to act as a self-fulfilling prophecy, so that children in lower streams, particularly those who were misplaced, did much worse than they might otherwise have done. It was also noticed that children of the manual working class were once again underrated and tended to congregate in dispro-portionate numbers in the lower streams. In this way com-prehensives were not just failing to make up for disadvantages; they might actually be increasing social polarization.

The arrangement most diametrically opposed to streaming is mixed-ability teaching, in which, as the name implies, children of all abilities are taught in the same class. The aim is to allow each child to proceed at his own pace, working most of the time either individually or with a small sub-group of the class, and in consultation with the teacher rather than as a simple recipient of facts provided by the teacher. Very often this means answer-ing questions on duplicated worksheets made up in the indi-vidual schools to cover whatever topic is under discussion. The teacher circulates from group to group or from pupil to pupil, solving any difficulties, answering questions and generally stimulating the work. The teaching method is very similar to that used in most primary schools.

Because the children are kept together, rather than segregated by ability (or by some more or less fallible assessment of ability), there is a great deal of ideological steam behind this form of organization, and many of those who support comprehensives on social grounds believe it the *sine qua non* of equality of opportunity. The best guess is that about a third of all secondary schools in England and Wales now use mixed ability in the first year. This drops slightly in the second year and much more sharply in the third (when many of the more-able children may start a second foreign language). Probably only about 2 per cent of schools have anything approaching mixed ability in the fourth and fifth years. The main reason for this is that the separate existence of G.C.E. and C.S.E. means there are almost inevitably two separate routes through school – one for the more academic children, one for the less. Once again, those who believe in equality of opportunity and social unification deplore the onset of selection by ability as soon as exams appear on the horizon (it is often described as a delayed eleven-plus). A drive towards a unified system of examining at sixteen-plus, and fierce opposition to it on practical and ideological grounds, and because of the implied extension of teacher power, has been one of the most significant developments in the 1970s. The topic is discussed in more detail in subsequent chapters.

Equally important has been the question of whether or not mixed-ability teaching really works, particularly in languages, mathematics and sciences. This too will be a subject for later discussion; but as background to that discussion, I should like at this point to offer a series of classroom snapshots. I have chosen English, since mixed-ability teaching is marginally less controversial here than in some subject areas, and once again I have chosen a London school. This is because it is generally believed in education circles that London has swung more sharply towards mixed-ability teaching than any other part of England or Wales.

Abbey Wood Comprehensive

The school in question is Abbey Wood Comprehensive, on the extreme south-east edge of the Inner London Area. There are 1350 pupils, making it a biggish place, and almost all of them are drawn from one, huge, housing estate. This means that Abbey Wood is a genuine neighbourhood school, though very short on middle-class children.

Many schools try to ensure that a single educational philosophy prevails throughout, and this has recently been endorsed as one of the trademarks of a school in good working order.[9] The philosophy of Charles Stuart-Jervis, head of Abbey Wood, is that each department should work to its own strength. Teaching in maths, science and home economics is fairly controlled and rigid, he told me when I visited the school, but in English it is far more liberal. The school is obtaining results 2 and 3 per cent above the national average in each of the English examinations taken. 'I'm convinced that this overall growth would not have been achieved without mixed ability,' says Mr Stuart-Jervis, 'and that's partly because the staff are convinced. I accept the view that either of the systems can work if the teachers are sufficiently committed.'

Abbey Wood rather tentatively offers exam results as an objective indication that all is well with the English department. But Danny Padmore, head of the department, seems more inclined to rate the department's success by the strength of creative writing. This theme, I discover, is quite as important as the stress on mixed ability and is in fact interwoven with it. But mixed-ability teaching in its purest form prevails in the first three years only. At the end of the third year the thirty or so who may be expected to take 'O' level are separated out. The remainder are taught in mixed-ability groups. 'Obviously, if we could, we would like to see the end of "O" level altogether,' says Padmore. 'The problem is the divisiveness. But there's no doubt the parents want it. There would be an outcry if we stopped.'

The mixed-ability arrangement for the others is comparatively recent. Six years ago, the third year was streamed into eight divisions. Since the change, exam results have remained constant, no better, no worse. 'But there has certainly been an improvement in the school,' says Padmore, 'and many of the problems of six years ago no longer exist. There used to be a group of disadvantaged kids who recognized themselves as such and went round together more or less chanting "We are the thickies – we rule". Now there has been an improvement in the social mix, an interaction of kids of different ability in the one classroom. This is something we value. I believe in mixed ability because I don't believe you can really distinguish in the way you must with streaming. It's to do with whether or not you want a fairer society or are prepared to continue in a stratified society. And don't let anybody fool you into thinking education isn't political, however it's presented. It either lends its support to the *status quo* or seeks to modify it.

'But I don't pretend there aren't lots of problems with mixed ability. Of course there are. The argument is that you are spending so much time with the slow kids the bright ones don't develop as much as they might. Well, of course that's a danger. A tremendous amount depends on the teacher, his awareness, experience and preparation. Another thing, the success of mixed ability depends on the ability of the teacher to form individual relationships with the kids. You'd be surprised how often that doesn't happen in schools. People don't bother or the pressures are too great. The point is that children develop at their own pace and a teacher has to know where a child is, in terms of his own creative personality. Much of this development doesn't take place anywhere near the classroom and you need an extraordinary teacher to understand and keep up with it.

'There used to be a tradition in the department of holding children back after school for individual talks, just on a casual basis. We have had a number of staff changes recently, but I hope the tradition is building up again.'

As with many people involved in mixed-ability teaching, the idealism is unmistakable. Here are my notes on what I actually saw in the classroom.

Third-year Group, Mixed Ability

This is a library period and Danny Padmore is the teacher. The children, who haven't yet quite lost the innocence that characterizes primary schools, take their seats – after three requests – in a room adjoining the library. Then they go in and change their books for the impending school holiday. One girl says she changes hers just to look good, she doesn't really read. But many have genuinely read the books they are returning. These are not all worthy volumes. They range from 'pop' science fiction and love stories to gritty tales of urban adventure (a kind of book which is currently much in fashion). Where a book is 'good' in the improver's sense, it is usually exciting as well. The first aim is pleasurable reading.

I scrutinize some of the children's writing books. Many mistakes are left uncorrected. Danny Padmore explains: 'I don't think it's any good going through a piece of writing and putting a red scribble through every line. The kid'll probably look at it and think "My God" and throw it away. It makes sense to the kid, though, if he thinks, "Oh there's something wrong with my speech marks".'

What about such 'basic skills' as grammar, punctuation and spelling? 'These can't be separated from the content,' Padmore replied. 'You can't say there's basic skills on one side and creative writing on the other, and work away at them separately. In our guidelines [a bulky, typewritten document] the emphasis is on creative writing. The main thing we have to do at the beginning is get the kids to *write* – about themselves, their feelings, their friends.'

I ask a group in the library how well Mr Padmore knows them. 'Oh, really well,' says a spokesman, 'he's had us for three years.'

Fourth-year C.S.E. Group

'Do you want to read?' the teacher asks.

'No,' drawls the fifteen-year-old pupil, 'not really.' The voice is lacklustre, inclining to rudeness. The teacher accepts the tone without remonstrance or even surprise. The pupil slouches, looks out of the window, after a moment picks up idle conversation with the other three boys who inhabit the same island of desks. Elsewhere among the islands there is a varied pattern of activity and inactivity. At one island, four girls are talking about a television programme as a preliminary to writing about it; some pupils are already writing, others seem simply to be passing the time. The teacher moves from group to group, reading their work, talking, cajoling, taking each child individually. It is all very low-key. The walls are mostly bare, in some places peeling. The atmosphere of off-handedness among some of the pupils is very strong.

But it emerges that the boy who didn't want to read has in fact written continuously for fifty minutes about hawks, a subject he has chosen for himself. No compulsion was involved. It also emerges that he is a pupil of low ability, one who might, under less encouraging circumstances, have written nothing at all. Each pupil has a folder of work. There is an impressive quantity of writing in almost all of them, some of it of a high quality, some of it the reverse. But everybody, it seems, has been writing copiously. What appeared at first sight a depressing and frankly disordered environment is in fact a productive one.

There seem to be two main elements in this. The first concerns order. This teacher gets most of what she wants by allowing her fourth-year class to have a good deal of what *it* wants – freedom to chat and a minimum of 'Yes, sir, no sir, three bags full, sir'. There is a kind of negotiated peace at a level a little shocking to those accustomed to a formal classroom atmosphere. But it is productive because the teacher knows how far she can go and stops any turbulence far short of riot. Several children confide in me during the day, saying things like, 'Mr So-and-So is fine. He keeps us in order. But have you heard about Mr

Topsy-Turvy in such and such a department. Some of the boys sing all the way through his class.' This is a theme a visitor encounters in almost every secondary school, whether independent or maintained.

Mr Stuart-Jervis, headmaster, comments: 'Children take a simplistic view. They didn't want to come to school, and if the teachers can't control them, they'll give them hell. If they can, then the children will be pleased about it.' The fourth-year class I'm visiting is under control despite a deceptive appearance.

The other important point is that the children are working from interest. This morning's writing involves free choice of subjects. But the main topic of the term has been chosen for them by the teacher. The subject is 'breaking away from home'. Each member of the class has been asked to invent a teenage character who leaves home and then to follow this character's progress through fictional but plausible situations. The process is aided by discussion, films and books. From it there springs much imaginative writing; some formal or functional writing (in what the jargon makers refer to as the 'transactional mode' – in this case it could be an exchange of letters over the rental of a room between two of the characters in the drama); writing about books; and writing about films. Writing in all these categories must be presented in the folders which, in eighteen months' time, will be the main basis for assessment in C.S.E. The project is chosen because it will touch each individual closely. It offers the children a chance to write about themselves, their own society, its pains, joys and problems, whether personal or social. The hope is that imaginative writing will flow, and that other forms of writing will flow from that.

There is no doubt that the result of this approach is an outpouring of imaginative writing at all levels of the school. Numerous magazines are produced and quite often the work of an individual is duplicated and stapled into a makeshift volume. Some of the writing is indifferent, but much is surprising and frequently moving. Only lack of space prevents me from providing example upon example, not just to prove my point but for the intrinsic worth of the writing. Many of the poems are in stanza form and rhyme, reflecting in this way both pop songs and the traditional ballad. That this is encouraged by the department shows, I think, a genuine awareness of what children love in language and poetry. Very often, under the banner of creative writing, totally uncontrolled effusions parade as poetry, the teachers having themselves acquired a wrong-headed view of the nature of contemporary poetry.

Homework is set regularly for the fourth year but only about half of it is done.

Another Fourth-year C.S.E. Group – Padmore Again

For a biggish chunk of this period, Mr Padmore reads out the last part of *The Triple Echo*, a story by H. E. Bates. So far as I can tell, he secures the attention of each individual. 'It's myth that mixed-ability teaching means nothing but individual work. You have to do a fair amount of whole-class teaching or the thing falls apart.'

Fifth-year C.S.E. Group

This class is watching a film. It's a difficult and rather highbrow drama of the American Civil War. Much violence, also some use of surrealism to suggest mental disorientation. Complex shifts in time sequence. Equally complex use of music. One or two students visibly disaffected, most apparently engaged. Films play a big part in the work of the English department, and may range from this kind of thing to box-office hits such as *The Sting* or *Butch Cassidy and the Sundance Kid*. Neil Galbraith, the teacher, says: 'Kids are fantastically knowledgeable about films and deeply involved with moving images. These impinge in all kinds of ways we don't usually tease out.' His notes for the lesson show he will later be asking questions about the story-line and others about the intentions of the makers, students at Britain's National Film School. What were they trying to do, for instance, by simply using stills and music at the beginning?

Upper Sixth

Sociology, as it happens, but Neil Galbraith is teacher. This class is a partial example of the 'new' sixth form, an increasingly important phenomenon. Where entry is open, as it is at Abbey Wood, a sixth form will probably contain students who came to it via C.S.E. and may not in fact be doing – or able to do – 'A' levels. In many schools these students may do 'O' levels or be dragged along rather unsatisfactorily in the wake of 'A' level candidates, their course distorted by the requirements the universities make of the minority. An alternative, somewhat less academic, exam, the C.E.E. or Certificate of Extended Education, is sometimes offered experimentally at seventeen. Some believe that it is having a liberating effect on the curriculum, others, that it is simply a further instance of the proliferation of exams. But Abbey Wood believes in it for many of the same reasons that it believes in C.S.E.

The present group are eighteen-year-olds. All are aiming at 'A' level (there are seven of them) but some did C.S.E., not 'O' level. How has this affected them, I ask? 'Well,' says one, 'it's such a different kind of work that the changeover is hard. In "A" level English, the examiners are not that interested in your creative writing. They want to know if you know all about the texts.'

Do they enjoy 'A' level work? Oh yes indeed, replies another. 'Before the sixth form you only do the work because it's set. But we are in the sixth form now because we want to be.' In *Oryx*, the sixth form magazine, the flow of imaginative writing, even if the writing is a little more self-conscious, is as profuse as lower down the school.

Even in the Abbey Wood English department, and despite the strong belief in mixed-ability teaching, there are, as we have seen, divisions by ability in the fourteen-to-sixteen age-range.

The vast majority of schools choose a path somewhere between streaming and mixed ability. One of the most common arrangements of all is banding,[10] a system by which a school may be divided into two or three, often with setting inside the divisions in subjects such as maths, science and languages.

Prince Henry's High School in Evesham, in the former county of Worcestershire, follows this pattern. In some respects it is untypical – notably in that it is a thirteen-to-eighteen school, the third tier in a system of primary, middle and high schools. But its catchment area of small country town and countryside is probably at least as representative as Abbey Wood's of a nation in which town and suburb increasingly outweigh the cities. And like many schools, Prince Henry's is in a state of considerable flux. It began to reorganize in 1973, converting itself stage by stage from an eleven-to-eighteen coeducational grammar school to a thirteen-to-eighteen comprehensive with a full cross-section of the ability range. Luckily for Prince Henry's, the school is all on one site. But in terms of age of pupil taught and nature of pupil intake, no two years have been the same since 1973. Nor will they be until 1980.

This continual change gives the teachers at Prince Henry's a sharp awareness of the pros and cons of going comprehensive. Many of them naturally see it from the point of view of former grammar school teachers adjusting to the needs of children of lower ability. In a 'converting' secondary modern the problem would be the accommodation of brighter children. But in a real sense, these problems are parallel, for they involve the abandonment of specialization in favour of the attempt to do one's best by children of every ability and background. The need to be all things to all pupils is the dominant feature of the comprehensive system.

I am certainly not offering Prince Henry's as typical – in our diverse system, there is no such thing as a 'typical' school. But in the following sketch of a day in the classroom there, I hope to pick up some themes which will be generally relevant to all schools and their pupils. One point, though, should be made clear to start with. Much of the description which follows deals with banding. This is dictated by the terms of the discussion and not because it obtrudes at every point. In practice, great efforts are made to divert attention from it. Classes are known by the initials of the teacher and banding applies to nothing except the actual lessons.

Prince Henry's High School, Evesham

A grey December day. Streets of brick-built houses edge up to the school on two sides; on the third, playing fields and a railway embankment; on the fourth, allotments and wintry orchard. The so-called third- and fourth-year pupils – aged from thirteen to fifteen – are present at assembly. (There are no eleven- or twelve-year-olds; the thirteen-year-olds have only just joined the school; but to avoid confusion the normal terminology of eleven-to-eighteen schools is used.) There's a fine, bold Christmas tree and a middling-lusty rendering of 'Hark the Herald Angels Sing'. At the first word of the final chorus, drums and cymbals strike up, loud and unexpectedly, and a wave of giggles goes through the throng. Almost all are tidily dressed – blazers, trousers, shirts and skirts all uniform, ties right up to the neck. Headmaster Stanley English wears a gown, concludes his part of the proceedings with a prayer of St Theresa's: 'Oh Lord, let us not live to be useless'. (In having a daily act of worship, Prince Henry's is one of a minority. Latest figures reveal that most schools don't – despite a clause in the 1944 Education Act making this compulsory for all schools with a hall big enough to assemble everybody at one time.) The prayers are followed by announcements and then the pupils file out, a fraction boisterously, but without the pushing and shoving that takes place at lunchtime outside the dining hall. This latter scene of hurly-burly is basically a good-natured contest between fifth-form boys and the master in charge. In the playgrounds at break-time, the atmosphere is exuberant rather than rough and not at all threatening. Fights, the continual nightmare in inner-city schools, are infrequent at Prince Henry's. 'We are still pretty self-contained and backward – thank God,' says Stanley English.

After assembly, pupils disperse to the five or six buildings on the rather jumbled site. None of these is ancient though the school was founded in 1377 and refounded in 1605. One is new and well-respected by pupils. 'Nobody else has scribbled on the walls, so they don't feel inclined to,' says a teacher. Another building is a long-outdated 'temporary' structure, leaky and decayed. The remainder are old-fashioned, scruffy but serviceable. A new arts centre, for school and community, is rising at one corner of the campus and there is plenty of mud about.

The pupils are divided into two broad bands before they arrive, on the basis of consultations between Prince Henry's and the feeder middle schools. About 10 per cent are reallocated sometime before their first Christmas at the school. (These, remember, are the equivalent of third-year pupils at an eleven-to-eighteen comprehensive. By this stage almost all schools operate banding or streaming.) Within the bands, there is setting by ability, in science, maths and languages. On banding, Stanley English says: 'A large number of staff had worked here when we were an old-established and successful grammar school. We felt that to go in one jump from this to mixed ability would be a recipe for disaster, even if mixed ability were justified in absolute terms. Some people on the staff wanted fine streaming, but most of us felt there was no justification for setting so many barriers between people.' Prince Henry's, he says, is genuinely comprehensive in trying to do its best for all children of all abilities within a single school. But there is general agreement among the staff that some mistakes are made in banding. Stanley English comments: 'While everybody thinks there may be a mistake or two in their own subject, it's very hard to get general agreement from the staff as to which boy or girl we should actually move.'

The children register at the beginning and end of the day in mixed-ability 'forms', each of which has its own room. The hope is that this grouping, rather than the academically segregated teaching groups, will be a basis for the formation of friendships. One sixth-former tells me that this is what really happens. But classroom observation suggests that the children tend to make friends mainly among those of similar ability, and so seat them-

selves according to performance, unless otherwise directed by
the teacher. During the day described, I attended classes in biology and general sciences; mathematics; art, English and history. Here are some notes.

Biology

Doug Marshall, head of biology, takes the lower sixth through
a test paper they have done in preparation for an 'A' level
exam five whole terms away. He has marked it the night before.
He is explicitly drilling them for the exam ... 'One and two are
pure swot questions, but that's alright. That's part of it. These
are things you have to know.' ... He calls biology 'biol'. A
practical is a 'prac'. It is all good, old-fashioned-sounding stuff
addressed to youngsters who came in originally on selective
entry. But even this apparently traditional sixth form is not
what it would have been ten years ago. Most of the students
have reached it via an 'O' level in Nuffield biology.

'It's a hard course,' says Doug Marshall, 'but most of those
who come through are much, much better candidates. And
that's quite simply because they have got an inquiring attitude.'

The original Nuffield biology was published in 1966. A foreword addressed to teachers says that the course is '... designed
to foster a critical approach to the subject with an emphasis on
experimentation and enquiry rather than on the mere assimilation of fact. In terms of a conventional syllabus this means
that less factual matter is included ...' A foreword to the pupil
says, in part: 'Experiments are not intended to prove things you
already know; they are to investigate whether something does
or does not happen so that you can form hypotheses which,
themselves, can be tested by further experiment ...' This is very
different from carrying out an experiment which proves that
what the teacher has already told you is correct.

The text itself deals, excitingly, with the history of discovery
and provides a lively and relevant-looking basis for the pupils'
own experiments. It is backed by illustrations that arouse genuine interest – in a chapter on movement, for example, a series of

pictures showing an athlete collapsing in an Olympics race from oxygen deprivation. One London headmaster, a classicist, told me he had never understood quite how radical Nuffield was until the day he stopped a boy from running on the stairs. 'Oh, sir,' he said, 'you've *ruined* my experiment. I'm checking the connection between pulse rate and the use of energy.'

Doug Marshall says that Nuffield provided a big public boost for an approach to science that was coming in piecemeal. Since then, all syllabuses in all sciences have been modified, with more and more emphasis on practical work as a path to true understanding. 'But it has its snags, no doubt about it,' he says. These lie in its comparative difficulty (see General Science, below).

General Science – One of the Bottom Groups of Third-year B Band

There's a buzz of excitement. Children in ones and twos are heating test tubes over bunsen burners and exclaiming as the metals inside react; others are burning metals on crucible lids, or watching what happens to them in combination with water or acid. Almost all the children are doing something slightly different, having reached different stages in a series of simple experiments.

'It's lovely,' says Mary. Like most of the girls she has a biro-drawn heart on the inside of her hand, in this case bearing the legend, 'Tommy is ace'. 'We do all these experiments and find things out,' she says. Excitedly, she shows me in her exercise book what she has written about an earlier experiment. In this, a trolley was allowed to run down a slope with a ticker-tape trailing behind it. A device at the top of the slope made dots on the ticker-tape at an even tempo. 'You see, the dots were close together when it was going slow, they were further apart when the trolley was going fast.' She has made a rudimentary bar-graph showing patterns of acceleration, deceleration and constant speed.

Other children communicate the same excitement. One boy tells me he makes up his own experiments: 'I've only done two of the right ones today.' Few have got very far with the work that has been set; but time is running out. Reluctantly, the teacher, Ken Morris, embarks on a blackboard summary: 'I'm not very happy writing this when we've only looked at two or three metals, that's not very scientific. But what we *can* say . . .'

'My feeling with a B band,' he says later, 'is that they enjoy the practical work but don't learn much from it. In this lesson I'm not trying to get any of the deep principles out. In Nuffield you would do experiments to draw out some fundamental point. You wouldn't tell your students anything they could reasonably find out by their own simple experiments. The difficulty is that with most pupils, it's asking too much of them to expect them to interpret their results. Here all I'm looking for is patterns – in the hope, say, that those going on with chemistry next year will remember that all metal carbonates give off carbon dioxide under suitable conditions. I want the generalizations on chemical behaviour rather than the theoretical explanations.

'They certainly enjoy themselves and there's a good class atmosphere, but I don't know how important that is.'

English – Fourth-year B Band

In terms of teaching-tactics, the most important fact about this and almost every class at Prince Henry's is that the children are taught throughout the lesson as a single group. In this class, sarcasm is the weapon used on late arrivals, and the butts of the sarcasm are docile enough to put up with it.

'It's difficult at the start with fourth years,' the teacher says afterwards, 'but by the end of two years you have got a strong relationship with them. They may not like you. They may still say "good" if you say you are feeling ill, but for them the value is in the familiarity. The familiarity is a bridge. What may have begun as a slanging match turns into give and take. And in this school there isn't any antipathy to the teaching staff. I've worked in Birmingham and Redditch and I was desperate to get back here . . .'

The approach to written work is very different from that at

Abbey Wood. The term has started with the use of practical or
'transactional' English – a project involving invitations to a
party followed by replies. Then the class did a story about
something that had gone wrong at the party. From here, the
teacher had tried to move on to more personal terrain, asking
the children to write a fantasy about the achievement of a great
ambition. The idea was based in part on a B.B.C. television
series running at the time. 'Television is something they can
really relate to,' said the teacher. Several of the girls had opted
for a motor-bike ride and candle-lit dinner with Barry Sheene;
several of the boys had played football for England or Leeds
United.

Discussing this piece of work in class, the teacher reveals her
eagerness that all shall be correctly written: 'You were so carried away by what you were saying that you didn't think how
you were saying it.' She tells them that too many sentences had
begun with 'then'; there were too many 'gots'. Next she sets
them to write half a page of 'got' sentences – 'I got my breakfast and got to the bus stop' – and then translate these into
more formal speech. 'You can talk as you like,' she tells the
children 'but when you are writing you have to be more
formal.' All the mistakes in all the exercise books are punc-
tiliously corrected in red. All homework is eventually done,
says the teacher, even if handed in late. To my eye the writing is
reasonably accurate but generally unadventurous. Verbal response seems minimal. The teacher agrees. 'As a group, they are
rather lifeless. Oral lessons are doomed to failure.'

A fifth-year A Band class which I attended seemed to bear
this out. An uninspired reading by the class of J. M. Barrie's
The Admirable Crichton was followed by a session in which the
teacher struggled hard to elicit any sort of response from the
pupils. Despite this, he was confident that they had understood
the play and that their written work on it would be passable.

Throughout the English department, the aim is to saturate
the children in books, on the theory that delight in the written
word will father a vigorous and creative use of English. This,

rather than personal feelings and experience as at Abbey Wood, is reckoned the best starting point, particularly for less-able children. 'They do not have the experience to draw on or the imaginative power,' says Lauri Griffith-Jones, the head of the department. 'This is what worries me about using creative writing as the starting point. That's fine with the A band but the B band need a lot more feeding.' Formal grammar teaching – parsing and analysis of subordinate clauses – is frowned upon. Each classroom has a library of 100 or so volumes and the turnover of textbooks is rapid. One period a week is devoted to silent reading. Another is set aside for drama.

Upper Sixth, a Group of Nine – Two Boys and Seven Girls

The subject is Milton's *Paradise Lost*. Only Book One has been set for the exam, but the group has ranged much further into Milton's enormous epic. To start with, Lauri Griffith-Jones, their teacher, read out loud to them quite frequently, hoping to convey his own enthusiasm and something of the flow and sonority of the language. Today the sixth-formers are taking it in turn to read. They have reached the point where Eve discloses her 'fatal trespass' to Adam.

> From his slack hand the garland wreathed for Eve
> Down dropt, and all the faded roses shed.

'Have you noticed the hand imagery?' asks Lauri Griffith-Jones. 'There's a marvellous concentration on hands running right through this poem. If you were making a film, this is an image you'd be picking up continually.'

The students agree; they have noticed the imagery, or some of them have, at least. And they have noticed, too, the image of drunkenness, used to describe Adam's state of mind when he has eaten the forbidden fruit. 'Everything destroyed but feeling marvellous,' says Lauri Griffith-Jones.

'Milton's tremendous,' said one of the girls. 'We'd heard he was terribly difficult but it's not like that at all. I would have looked forward to it if I'd known.'

But what I heard her saying was something slightly different: that, contrary to the popular myth, there exists within the maintained system, to be found perhaps in every town and city, the kind of delight in our literary culture that enables a teacher to transcend the difficulties and communicate his joy to students who could not at this age have made very much on their own of a writer like Milton. For Mr Griffith-Jones the test will come as the composition of the sixth form changes. But the transmission of delight in the written word will remain one of his duties.

Problems, though, as always. One of the group tells me later that fewer and fewer people are prepared to sign their poetry in the 'Henrician', the school magazine. Another sixth-former says: 'There's a bit of an atmosphere creeping in that those who do well at exams and so forth are doing the wrong thing.' But a reading of the 'Henrician' certainly does not suggest a collapse in creativity. The maligned junior years seem to me adequately represented.

Third-year Maths – A Band

Only eagerness on show. I don't know whether to believe the gloomy sixth former. Brisk, all-class teaching, of a kind that would be familiar to any parent who had started on trigonometry – tangents, cotangents, angles, minutes and degrees. The whole class moves on step by step together, the only difference being that some of them – in this case a group of boys – speed through the exercises and need a little extra work to be given them by the teacher as he moves about the room.

Two girls tell me that it's not competitive and that they enjoy the work. But there is a dark tale of a maths teacher in another class who couldn't do a sum and had to go for help. (For more on the desperate shortage of qualified maths teachers, see 'The teachers', Chapter Four.)

All the maths at Prince Henry's is broadly traditional so that, for parents, there are few of the difficulties in understanding what is happening that are so often attendant on the 'new maths'. But Eric Tyler, head of maths in the school, makes an important point in conversation. The basic thing to grasp, he says, is that in mathematics, in sharp contrast, say, to geography and science, no great revolution in intellectual approach has occurred. What has changed is that various new methods of computation and calculation have arrived. Among the most important of these are binary mathematics where, instead of the digits 0 to 9, only 1 and 0 are used. This is a kind of language that is easily used by computers, a fact which gives binary mathematics great practical significance. But the basic numerical concepts that are expressed remain exactly the same. So also with 'sets' and 'matrices', two of the other best-known elements of modern maths. These, too, involve a different way of ordering and expressing the units involved in calculation. But basically, they only help you solve the kind of problems which you might otherwise have solved by simultaneous equations.

All these methods of calculation remain highly controversial because there is no agreement over whether or not they actually make the solution of problems easier. Modern maths, most notably in the shape of S.M.P., the Schools Mathematics Project pioneered by Professor Bryan Thwaites, made great progress for a decade or so but S.M.P. is now somewhat on the retreat, leaving behind it, most typically, a mixed pattern in which schools try to use the best of both systems.

Third-year Maths – B Band

'Dusty' Rhodes, the teacher, has come to Prince Henry's by way, among other things, of a London comprehensive, a school in Canada and a Worcestershire secondary modern. He brought with him the essence of a Mode III C.S.E. syllabus now called, at Prince Henry's, 'Arithmetic, money management and statistics'. The arithmetic involved in this course is, as in the rest of the school, generally traditional, but the content is radically different from anything that I at least was ever asked to do at school. On the syllabus I see references to bus and train timetables, hire purchase, gas and electricity bills, and savings. One project involves planning a holiday, with a choice of costing out a package holiday abroad or a self-catering holiday in this country. Another involves helping to operate the school Savings Bank, then writing about its organization and the part the pupil has played. Yet another involves costing a piece of do-it-yourself carpentry, dressmaking or catering for a dinner party.

Rhodes says: 'It sounds a lot more fun than it actually is. The students are not over-responsive to work and this means the course is of less value to them than it might be.'

The class is cheerful and talkative. Relationships are evidently good but there is tremendous variation in the neatness and success rate of different pupils. Mr Rhodes drifts about, teaching individually, as the pupils chat and, sometimes, work. I hear him on the far side of the room discussing Tchaikovsky. A girl tells me that she hates one of the text books: 'The pictures are babyish. It's boring. It's so simple it's embarrassing to carry about. I sandwich it between two other books.' I ask one of the boys whether he would like to be in the A band for mathematics. 'Oh no,' he says, 'they do really boring work in those classes.'

Art

In its grammar school days, Prince Henry's concentrated on drawing and painting, in a course leading in the first instance to an 'O' level exam. This has now broadened out to include batik, work with clay, silk-screen printing, lino printing and so on. But art, along with gymnastics, feels itself the poor relation. 'Of course, if we were purpose built,' a teacher tells me, 'these two subjects would be bumped up.' This situation seems fairly general where old grammar schools have been converted. Art, drama and music, often the glory of through-and-through comprehensive education, are squeezed by lack of space and sometimes by an over-academic approach. Metal and woodwork, too, can sometimes suffer from lack of funds and prestige. At Prince Henry's the craft side is now being built up. A larger proportion of B band children tend to take the practical subjects. In a jaundiced moment a metal-work teacher says of them: 'They use the materials as weapons. You have to watch it.' In secondary moderns going comprehensive, the problem is not the craft side but finding the qualified mathematicians and assembling an adequate sixth-form library.

English Faculty Meeting

This meeting, one of a series held every few weeks, lasts from four till five-thirty (school ends at three-forty). The issue of banding comes up and somebody suggests three streams instead of two. 'Those of us who taught 3M would oppose that tooth and nail,' one teacher says, referring to an unsuccessful experiment in the past. Another refers, in carefully neutral tones, to a school elsewhere in Worcestershire where a 'C' stream is 'kept down by heavy discipline'.

'The people who would be in that "C" stream are very much better off under our present system,' says Lauri Griffith-Jones. The real business of the meeting, however, is to ratify the head of department's decision to set up a Mode III C.S.E. course for 'B' band English. In this, assessments will be based on a folder of work done over two years and there will be no exam at all. Mr Griffith-Jones makes a short, quite formal speech: 'We as a school, society in general, have not done as well by these children as we ought to have done ... we know the kind of showing the "B" band will make in a Mode I exam; we know they are often not able to learn and regurgitate the material for the exam ... As I have said before, I have very little respect for the C.S.E. Mode I. Though it's set by professionals and should be alright, it's slackly moderated and the content sometimes leaves a lot to be desired ... If we do our own Mode III, it will mean a lot more work; but it will have more integrity. That's something I feel quite strongly about.'

Prince Henry's remains a broadly traditional school, committed to the transmission of values which are often thought to be disappearing. There are many hundreds of schools which adopt a similar approach. One of the most interesting points to note, however, is that even traditional schools are prepared to innovate on behalf of the less able. Teachers see this as a way both of improving the pupils' prospects and of making their school life worthwhile from day to day. And if there is one overall impression which I hope this chapter will have conveyed it is that modern teaching methods are often practised by serious people with a strong sense of social responsibility.

Notes

1. Bowie, Janetta, *Penny Buff* (Constable, 1975).
2. Schwebel, Milton, and Ralph, Jane (eds) *Piaget in the Classroom* (Routledge and Kegan Paul, 1974).
3. Pluckrose, Henry, *Open School, Open Society* (Evans Brothers, 1975).
4. Bennett, S. N., and Jordan, J., 'Teaching Styles in Primary Schools', *British Journal of Educational Psychology*, vol. 45 (1975).
5. Wright, Nigel, *Progress in Education* (Croom Helm, 1977).
6. Her lengthy articles appeared on 11 February 1977 and 18 February 1977.
7. Dore, Ronald, *The Diploma Disease: education, qualification and development* (Allen and Unwin, 1977).
8. See 'Teaching Geography' – a Digest, published on 18 June 1976 by *Education*, at that time the journal of the Association of Education Committees, now published by Councils and Education Press Ltd.
9. *Ten Good Schools*, H.M.I. Series: 'Matters for Discussion', No. 1, 1977.
10. See above p. 33 for discussion of banding in the alternative sense of the equal distribution throughout the school system of children of all abilities.

3. The counter-revolution

Between the Plowden Report in 1967 and Mr Callaghan's speech in 1976, the opponents of progressive education found a voice and used it effectively to sway public opinion. My hope in this chapter is to describe that process and to give some account of the ideas, events and personalities that contributed to it.

The main figure-head of the counter-revolution has undoubtedly been Dr Rhodes Boyson, Conservative M.P. for Brent and a Black Paper editor since 1975. Dr Boyson's strength is that he has been headmaster of a northern secondary modern, of a London comprehensive and of a London grammar school which converted to comprehensive; his seemingly bluff, right-wing approach to education is matched by a right-wing stance on moral issues. He is, for example, heavily in favour of national exams at seven, eleven and fourteen – an essential part of the Tory plan for 'tightening up' – and bitterly opposed to the advertisement of contraceptives. This populist combination, along with personal affability and a passion for political cut-and-thrust, has made him something of a national figure. But more can be learned of the *intellectual* development of the counter-progressive movement from the career and writings of Brian Cox, Professor of English at Manchester University and the only person to have been involved throughout as a Black Paper editor. Professor Cox's career has been marked by growing moral doubt, leading him finally to a rejection of the main literary and artistic developments of the last fifteen or twenty years; and this is one of the strongest shaping forces behind the Black Papers.

Cox, who has held his university chair for almost a decade, was born fifty years ago in a working-class district in Grimsby.

After a grammar school education – not, he says, a good one – and before completing his doctorate at Cambridge, he worked both at a secondary modern school and as an army instructor dealing mainly with illiterates. There, he says, he learnt 'how difficult it was'. As a convinced Labour supporter he also gave evening classes for the Workers' Educational Association. Then in 1958, while somewhat underemployed at Hull University, he and his colleague Tony Dyson decided to produce a new cultural journal to be called the *Critical Quarterly*. Both men had been pupils of Dr F. R. Leavis at Cambridge and now wanted, Cox wrote,[1] 'to turn literary criticism away from puritanism towards intelligent celebration of creative achievement'. They believed it was 'worth devoting a life to presenting, teaching, and celebrating great art' and their aim – a large one – was 'to ensure that high standards of lucid English and a wide appreciation of great literature remained powerful elements of our common culture'. This meant that along with critical articles they published a substantial number of new poems. Many of these, by writers ranging from Philip Larkin to Sylvia Plath, have now become well known, and Cox rates this as the main success of the *Critical Quarterly*.

But Cox quite early began to be critical of the 'Movement' poetry of the 1950s, arguing that the return to orthodox syntax and conventional stanza form had accompanied a withdrawal from the most agonizing areas of human experience. Yet in the early 1960s, when anarchic and anti-rational writing began, in their view, to dominate the English literary scene, Cox and Dyson were dismayed. 'As editors we could no longer feel optimistic that by promoting rational discussion of new literature we were contributing to a gradual and inevitable enlargement of a civilized community. We had to accept that we were increasingly in the position of a beleaguered minority, and that our duty in the future would involve more emphasis on the transmission of great literature of the past into the consciousness of present-day readers.'[2]

They were equally shocked by neo-Modernist art and at what they felt to be its random, indeterminate quality, sometimes suicidal in tendency, with the past perceived as an irrelevance and precise communication as impossible. Its concentration on immediacy and sensationalism were, they believed, the very negation of rational discourse. And yet it was this, in the form of 'pop' culture, which had come so to obsess the young that neither pupils, students nor many of their teachers appreciated that there was value in 'the life of the mind'.[8]

These gloomy reflections on culture were reinforced in 1964. Cox was at that time at Berkeley University in California and was present when students, fortified by Joan Baez singing 'We Shall Overcome', first turned to civil disobedience, setting a pattern for a decade of student militancy that spread rapidly to almost every country outside the Communist bloc. 'The original grievances of the students were entirely justified,' Cox told me during a series of conversations in 1976, 'but the thing got out of hand and this led to constant breaking of the law.' What had happened, he said, was that the students had discovered an easy way for minorities to impose their will and so to abuse the rights of the majority. From now on disruptions in the universities and the newly founded polytechnics seemed to Cox, and to many others who worked in them, a real threat to the values of 'high culture'.

As far as schools were concerned, the decisive shock for Cox came through his own children.

'When we got back from the States they had built a new school behind our house. There was every reason to assume this would be a marvellous place for the children. It took us about six weeks to realize it was a disaster area. No formal teaching went on at all and the children chose their own activities all day. My two elder children – then nine and six – were very unhappy. I think both of them wanted some order sometimes, as all children do. At the end of a year, in ordinary terms of achievement – literacy and numeracy – they had gone backwards.'

Month by month Cox and his wife – a secondary school teacher – became more outraged. 'You see, the idea that there would be no sequence, no structuring of any kind, came as a great shock. I had always approved, and still do, of discovery methods and teaching techniques that lead to self-reliance. But I had no idea there could exist in Britain so extreme a form of education as this. I think everyone now agrees there should be control, whether overt or covert. This was not so in 1965.'

Cox has a story, whether serious or not it's hard to tell, that there was a piano sitting in the school and nobody to teach the children how to play it. The idea was that children would learn for themselves if they were interested enough.

Walking on Hampstead Heath one winter's day, Cox and Dyson decided to devote the 1969 spring issue of *The Critical Survey*, an appendix to the *Critical Quarterly*, to a denunciation of student activism and a justification of the traditional view of the university. They began to solicit articles from writers and academics with whom they were in touch through the *Critical Quarterly*. Schools were an afterthought, added mainly because the attitudes implicit in modern education seemed to Cox and Dyson to offer some explanation of the student phenomenon. Thus we find them in the first Black Paper[4] quoting approvingly from an *Evening Standard* article by Timothy Raison, now a Conservative M.P., who had speculated that student unrest had its roots in 'the revolution in our primary schools'.

Today, with the virtual disappearance of the student revolutionaries, it seems probable that the years of protest were more closely linked to affluence, and that the Black Paper writers, in this respect at least, had picked the wrong reason for attacking modern practice in schools.

But the first Black Paper touched on another matter which does appear now, with the benefit of hindsight, to be linked to both progressive education and radical politics and so to be, from a right-wing standpoint, a proper target for criticism. This is the desire of students to have some say in what they are taught.

Kingsley Amis dealt with it briskly in the first Black Paper. 'A student, being (if anything) engaged in the acquiring of knowledge, is not in a position to decide which bits of knowledge it is best for him to acquire, or how his performance in the acquisition of knowledge can be assessed, or who is qualified to help him in this activity.'

Nevertheless, and despite Kingsley Amis, the claim is still being advanced, at school level as well as in higher education. It commands support among some liberal school-teachers. In educational terms, this support derives from the teachers' desire to make the best possible use of their pupils' own interest and of what they perceive as relevant. As such, it may represent little more than an extension of the teacher's role in answering questions (which almost all teachers, whether traditional or progressive, are delighted to do). In educational politics, however, it is associated with the neo-Marxist proposition that 'knowledge' cannot easily be separated from the socio-economic position of the person trying to impart it. Knowledge is 'relative' and value-laden, the theory runs; and if the political stance of students is more 'correct' than that of their teacher, then they will stand a better chance than he, of interpreting, say, history 'correctly'. If this is so, then they will also have some right to say what should be taught and how. Obviously, some matters are beyond dispute – the number of dead in a railway accident or the knowledge a surgeon needs to perform an operation – but subjects such as history and sociology are highly political, however one looks at them. A demand for a change in syllabus – to include, perhaps, an account of slavery in the Caribbean in a modern-history course – may involve the unspoken assertion of a neo-Marxist position, and the rejection of such a change, the unspoken rejection of that position; and, whichever side one is on, it is just as well to be clear about what is happening. In picking up this topic, the first Black Paper was prescient.

In technique, this first attempt at opinion-forming gave a good indication of the pattern the other Black Papers were to follow. It was a mixture of newspaper snippets and provocative 'think-pieces' written to express opinion rather than to present research, and it included an attempt to prove through statistics that comprehensives did less well by their pupils than the schools they were replacing. Its editorial, presented as a letter to Members of Parliament, was fiercely critical of 'the new fashionable anarchy' which 'holds that children and students will work from natural inclination rather than the desire for

reward' and 'like other anarchisms, tends to be more authoritarian than the system it seeks to replace'. Claiming that students didn't *know* as much as they should and endorsing a
report from the *Daily Mail* that illiteracy was growing, the
'Letter' commented: 'It is our belief that disastrous mistakes are
being made in modern education, and that an urgent re-
appraisal is required of the assumptions on which "progressive"
ideas, now in the ascendant, are based.'

This was good knock-about polemic, not done at any very
deep level, and hardly, one would have thought, the stuff of
counter-revolutions. It was Labour's Education Secretary,
Edward Short, who did the trick at the N.U.T.'s Easter conference by referring to the Black Paper's publication as 'one of
the blackest days for education in the past one hundred years'.
The 'backlash' it had provoked against progressive education
had created 'the crisis of this century', he said. Cox and Dyson
were immediately subjected to a torrent of press abuse.

'We were shattered,' Cox told me. 'We were literary men used
to being rude to one another in journals. But it was quite
different to wake up in the morning and find every newspaper
in the country calling us crackpots or Fascists.' Simultaneously
the Black Paper became an educational best-seller.

The editors' immediate response was to produce a second
Black Paper[5] in the same year and a third[6] in 1970. These,
though still in the same pamphleteering tradition, were more
substantial documents. Comprehensive schools and progressive
education, instead of student militancy, had now become the
main targets, and remained so in 1975[7] and 1977[8] when further
Black Papers were brought out under the joint editorship of
Cox and Boyson, Dyson having decided to concentrate on theo-
logy instead.

The Black Papers have proved enormously influential – if not
in their own right, then as presented by radio, press and television. In the early days, they were ridiculed by those who belonged to the prevailing liberal orthodoxy. It required some
courage to contribute a signed article and most of those who
wrote sympathetic letters, almost all of them teachers, asked for

their names to be withheld. But by the time of the 1977 Black Paper, a great many people were ready to listen to the case about the supposed plight of the bright, working-class child in a neighbourhood comprehensive or the argument in favour of setting a single, national exam for all children of a given age. The ideas remained extremely contentious but they were well within the ambit of public debate.[9]

How did this happen?

One reason advanced by Cox is that the Black Papers provided intellectual justification for views which were held secretly, almost guiltily, among many teachers – those who knew that 'informal methods were not working'.

A second reason for their impact is that many of the articles have been written by entertaining writers – among them Iris Murdoch, Kingsley Amis (four times so far), Robert Conquest, Patrick Moore and the gloomy American academic Jacques Barzun. The Black Papers are much more readable than most of the works produced by the other side.

Then there were the alarming statistics produced in the Black Papers to back the repeated assertion that standards were falling drastically and that both progressive methods and comprehensive schools were implicated in this. The development of their case here was much favoured by over-optimistic claims from the progressive side in the early days. Thus, for example, we find Lady Plowden, writing in the foreword to John Blackie's *Inside the Primary School*:[10] 'The new methods in the primary schools have shown how much more the child learns and how high can be his achievement if instead of being made to learn, the emphasis is on making him want to learn.' The reformers also produced sets of exam results purporting to show great improvements within a short time in reorganized secondary schools. This gave the Black Paper writers a considerable opportunity for polemic and they accepted it eagerly. Their facts and figures, however, have attracted much criticism.

Nigel Wright, an experienced teacher with a Cambridge degree in economics and prizes for his performance in the

theory and practice of teaching at London University's Institute
of Education, has recently spent eighteen months assessing the
weight of evidence on the main topics raised by the Black
Papers. This led him, inevitably, to test the accuracy of the
Black Papers themselves.[11] There were, he wrote in summarizing his soberly documented findings, 'an enormous
number of errors, inaccuracies, misrepresentations, con-
tradictions and confusions . . . As a contribution to serious educational debate the Black Papers are of limited value; as a
political battle-cry they are extremely stirring.' Despite their
limitations, many people have accepted as gospel the central
tenet of the Black Papers – that standards are falling dramatically.

Yet another possible reason for success is that the Black
Papers have helped polarize the debate, so that 'traditional' and
'progressive' have come to be seen as manichaean extremes of
light and darkness – or darkness and light, depending which side
one is on. This bears relatively little relationship to practice, for
many schools – and among them some of the best – are mixed
in what they actually do.

But while previously parents and general public had only a
rather vague idea that things were changing, the Black Paper's
opposition of progressive and traditional enabled them to take
up a sharply defined position, even if this was based on not much
more than caricature.

This is a point which takes a little proving, for a number of
the best Black Paper articles are in fact concerned with separating the good from the bad in progressive education and
even argue for retention of the former. Two examples are
J. W. G. Crawford's 'The Primary School: A Balanced View'
and G. H. Bantock's 'Discovery Methods', both in Black Paper
Two. The latter is an extremely impressive analysis of Rousseau's *Émile* in which Professor Bantock argues that discovery
methods can, in the end, be worthwhile only if subordinated to
the development of a coherent structure of ideas. Nor can they
be a permanent substitute for building on the findings of others
– one of the most important of human abilities, according to

Bantock. Their main use, he urges, is in arousing interest (in a way that goes well beyond 'the old formal methods'), in helping children 'to learn how to learn' and encouraging them to rely on their own initiative. Discovery methods, says Bantock, 'constitute an important but limited addition to the vocabulary of teaching.' But, he concludes: 'There is, in fact, no one way.'

All this seems admirably balanced and designed precisely to prevent over-simplification, but one of the most important points about the Black Papers is that the discourse is carried on simultaneously at quite different levels, so that while Bantock argues in this style in number two, in number one a primary headmistress, Miss C. M. Johnson, is writing: 'Some of my friends in junior schools tell me that marking and correcting is a thing of the past as it may bring a sense of failure to a child ... these children are growing up in a welfare state where it appears to them that everything in school is free; it is a world where they follow their own inclinations and where things are not right or wrong but merely a matter of opinion ... Never before have there been so many people mentally disturbed, and the official criminal statistics, issued by the Home Office, show that the greatest number of indictable offences recorded for males occurs in the fourteen and under seventeen age group ...'

While it is easy to praise Bantock (though hard to précis him), it is even easier for the media to make a meal – as they did – of the generalizations and juxtapositions of an article such as Miss Johnson's with its insinuation that progressive means permissive and that it is a short step from Plowden to the Old Bailey. It is in this way that the lower-level discourse of the Black Papers has had a greater impact than other more thoughtful Black Paper articles.

One important conclusion to be drawn from this success is that facts count for relatively little in deciding attitudes to education. The leader of a well-known educational trade union said to me recently during the dying stages of a party: 'Facts don't matter a fuck in education. It's my job to articulate the prejudices of my members. That's how you get things done.' And commenting on this, a senior H.M.I.[12] remarked: 'Mood is everything in education.' This may help to explain the success, first of Plowden, now of the Black Papers.

It is also undoubtedly the case that while most practice today stands somewhere between the extremes of 'pure progressivism' and 'pure traditionalism' there are quite different philosophies behind each. Professor Cox puts it this way: 'People divide themselves into two big groups, depending by and large on whether they see human nature as tending naturally towards kindness and love or, on the other hand, towards self-interest and greed. I'm firmly in the latter camp. I believe that society must impose order and a concept of service because these will not develop naturally.'[13]

This Hobbesian approach is currently heard a good deal from people in education and sometimes in an extraordinarily pessimistic form. Here are two examples from 1977: first, the headmaster of a girls' boarding school, who declared his belief in original sin on B.B.C. 'Woman's Hour', and then went on to quote with approval Jeremiah Chapter 17, Verse 9: 'The heart is deceitful above all things, and desperately wicked; who can know it?'; and second, the president of the N.A.S./U.W.T.,[14] Bernard Farrell, who said in his presidential address, a prepared oration printed in advance: 'People are killing for the sake of killing. Violence is a cult. Rape is for mere report and con- donation in the courts. Old women of eighty-five and babes five weeks old are subject to the same savage treatment. No-one is immune. No-where [sic] is safe . . . One might ask why all this should have evolved in the last twenty years or so. I believe the answer lies in ourselves. We have failed to recognize the dangers; we have allowed pretentious authority and expert opinion to indoctrinate us; we have trusted where we should have questioned, and evil is in control.'

This is considerably more extreme than Professor Cox, but it nevertheless seems clear that the Black Papers, springing as they do from cultural gloom allied to fear of anarchy in art and in the streets, occupy some of the same terrain as Mr Farrell. What matters for the future is how many people decide to join them. For while optimism and progressive methods are linked, so also are pessimism about human nature and a traditional approach.

Since the publication of the first Black Paper a number of events have taken place which have greatly encouraged Professor Cox and sympathizers, and in respect of which they are inclined either to take the credit or else to say 'I told you so'. Mr Callaghan's speech of October 1976 was evidently a response to the cumulative effect of these events as well as being one of them itself.

The first was the Start and Wells reading survey,[15] carried out in 1970 and 1971 and published in 1972. This suggested that while standards had been rising from a low, post-war base until about 1964, they had not continued to rise and, as recorded in one test, had actually declined. Despite the researchers' requests for caution, this finding caused a considerable uproar and was taken as confirmation that reading difficulties discovered in Kent in 1959[16] were prevalent throughout the nation. In the alarm that followed, Mrs Thatcher set up a committee under Lord (then Sir Alan) Bullock. While it was sitting, further research results appeared and were interpreted in some quarters as meaning that Welsh children, too, were in trouble over reading.[17] The Bullock Committee's massive volume of findings, produced in 1973, is generally known as the Bullock Report, but as there has now been a second Bullock Report, this time on industrial democracy, it is perhaps better to use its formal title, *A Language for Life*.

A Language for Life examined the evidence on reading standards and came up with a number of somewhat contradictory findings. The tests that had been used by Start and Wells, though at that time the best available, were not adequate measures of reading ability, the report said; the many practical difficulties acknowledged in Start and Wells (and in the Welsh research) implied severe limitations in the accuracy of the findings. Even so, the committee felt that there might now be 'a growing proportion of poor readers among the children of unskilled and semi-skilled workers' and that the national averages almost certainly masked falling reading standards in areas with severe social and educational problems. But at the same time, because of their low 'ceiling', the tests used gave little indication of the standards that were being reached by the best readers. The final conclusion of *A Language for Life* was this: 'The statistical results from the survey at both age points [eleven and sixteen] are not greatly disturbing, but neither do they leave room for complacency.' (Unfortunately for the peace of mind of those inclined to accept this summary, there was a dissenting note by Mr Stuart Froome, former headmaster and a Black Paper contributor, who rejected the report's interpretation of the statistics, asserted that standards were in fact declining and blamed discovery methods, emphasis on creativity and the concept of reading readiness – a notion going back some decades but now associated with Piaget's 'stages'. The charge here is that teachers wait for their pupils to mature instead of getting on with teaching them to read.)

The report devoted some quarter of a million words to ways in which the effective and pleasurable use of English might be developed in every phase of a child's life at home and school. This has proved highly influential,[18] so much so that some people concerned with mathematics believe a similar report might be effective in raising both issues and standards in that discipline. But in view of the controversy over standards in English and the unsatisfactory nature of existing evidence, the Bullock committee also recommended a new system of national monitoring of many different aspects of reading, writing and speaking. This would be done by sampling rather than by examining all children nationally. Even so, it was estimated that implementation of the proposals would cost about £100 million and long before the report was submitted – to Labour's Reg Prentice, who had now taken over from Mrs Thatcher – it was clear that expense of this order was just not possible. But the fact that the recommendation was made at all has come to assume significance in the era of the 'Great Debate'.

Another important event was the announcement a few months before Bullock reported that an 'Assessment of Performance Unit' was to be set up by the D.E.S. The function of this body would be to 'promote the development of methods of assessing and monitoring the achievement of children at school, and to seek to identify the incidence of under-achievement'. This implied something rather less elaborate than the monitoring called for in *A Language for Life*, but it was one more response to growing national anxiety over standards. The A.P.U. got to work extremely slowly and will not have much impact before the end of the decade. But I shall argue later that it may come to have a liberating rather than a restrictive influence.

While anxiety over standards grew apace, another issue was coming to the fore. This was violence and indiscipline in school. There has always been unruliness in school, as readers of history and biography will know, but now it began to receive concentrated attention. The N.A.S. issued a series of horrifying reports of teachers assaulted, kicked in the groin or face and generally confronted with uncontrollable violence. Though their 1975 study[19] made it quite clear that there was no evidence as to whether violence was actually increasing – because of the 'lack of objectivity and accuracy on the part of the teachers filling in the forms', said the foreword to the report – the impression conveyed to the public was undoubtedly that it was. Newspapers, both sensitive to public mood and helping to create it, began to emphasize horror stories and many of these found their way into such books as Dr Boyson's *The Crisis in Education.*[20] Though Dr Boyson did not actually say in so many words that school violence was growing, this was the clear implication of such remarks as: 'Adolescent violence has increased ten-fold in twenty years and it would be both difficult and naïve to absolve the schools of all responsibility.' By the end of 1977 the N.A.S./U.W.T. were asserting that decline in discipline was the single biggest factor in our educational problems, far outweighing any of the issues that the government had addressed itself to as a result of the Great Debate. At the same time the N.A.H.T., the National Association of Head Teachers (representing the heads of two-thirds of state schools), was particularly worried about the behaviour of younger children. Launching a campaign against 'bovver' belts with heavy clips and other potentially offensive items of clothing, the association said: 'We believe there is evidence to show an increasing anti-social activity among the under-tens. The law needs to be tightened up . . .' It was a shattering experience for a junior teacher, the statement went on, to 'find the classroom daubed with obscenities, the paint mixed on the floor with glue and water, pets and fish killed and mutilated, books torn and scribbled on'.

Pace the N.A.S. and N.A.H.T., there are in fact no reliable national figures to suggest that violence and vandalism are increasing. The only noteworthy indication that they may be is the fact that 1000 places in 'secure units' which existed before the Second World War have now disappeared. This means that there are a few more disruptive children than there were before in ordinary schools; and all agree that even a few disturbed children can make a great difference. But though one would expect this to have made its greatest impact in London, because of the concentration of social problems in the capital, no discernible impact has been felt. A paper on disruptive children, presented by Peter Newsam, I.L.E.A.'s education officer, in January 1978 said categorically that there was no evidence that bad behaviour in inner London schools was increasing: 'If anything, the reverse appears to be true.'[21]

Why, then, is there so firm an impression to the contrary? Obviously the N.A.S. are responsible to some degree. Another frequently proffered suggestion is that the professional classes, who exercise a disproportionate influence on what gets into the newspapers, are becoming conscious of school violence for the first time. This is because their children, formerly shielded by the grammar schools, now find themselves exposed in comprehensives to the kind of behaviour that took place unremarked in secondary moderns. There may be an element of truth in this. One should also be cautious about individual horror stories that seem to reflect on adolescents generally. By far the most authoritative account of adolescent *mores*, the National Child Development Study's survey[22] of sixteen-year-olds (based on research into the 16,000 children born in a single week in 1958), revealed that teenagers were in general thoroughly traditional in behaviour and beliefs. Most of them got on well with their parents, believed in marriage and had trouble at home only over such minor issues as dress and hair. (Drink, however, was a common problem.) Parents confirmed this generally peaceful picture. Teachers too gave their view of behaviour difficulties, and this was very different from the impression conveyed by Dr Boyson and the N.A.S. Asked whether the young people in the survey often destroyed or damaged their own or other people's property, the teachers said that this applied 'certainly' in only 1 per cent of cases, 'somewhat' in 5 per cent and did not apply in 93 per cent.[23] Asked whether the young people frequently fought or were extremely quarrelsome with other children, they said this applied 'certainly' in 2 per cent of cases, 'somewhat' in 8 per cent and did not apply in 90 per cent. This hardly suggests a generation on the rampage.

It is nevertheless clear that whether or not things are getting worse they are in some schools at some times exceedingly unpleasant. To this extent, the N.A.S. account may be accepted. Most cities have experienced school stabbings; schools built to be open to the community have sometimes had to be defended from marauding groups. Vandalism is also extensive. In the most careful review of evidence so far attempted, Judith Stone and Felicity Taylor[24] estimated that arson and other forms of vandalism were costing about £15 million a year and that in Glasgow alone repairs to wilfully damaged schools would build two new primaries a year.

Probably more important than this in the long run is widespread disaffection towards school. The sixteen-year-olds in the National Child Development Study were the first group who had to stay on at school after the leaving age was raised. They may have felt some resentment at this. Accordingly their answers should be treated with caution. Nevertheless, the degree of dissatisfaction was remarkable: 11 per cent thought school was largely a waste of time; 15 per cent said they never took work seriously; 36 per cent said they found it hard to keep their minds on work; 29 per cent said they did not like school and 54 per cent found homework a bore.

One factor in the dislike of school appears to be the use of corporal punishment. Forty-seven per cent of the sample thought it should never be used in school. But the report showed that it was used regularly or occasionally in 30 per cent of schools and 'very rarely' in another 42 per cent. In 1977 the Society of Teachers opposed to Physical Punishment (S.T.O.P.P.) claimed that while it was disappearing in some areas as a result of local government reorganization, it was reappearing in just as many others. The United Kingdom and Eire, S.T.O.P.P.'s secretary said, were the last countries in Europe to retain it.

Nobody can say for certain whether corporal punishment diminishes indiscipline in school or contributes to it. There is, however, some suggestion that rates of absenteeism (running at a steady national average of about 10 per cent) may drop and the general atmosphere improve in schools where steps are taken to reduce conflict between 'middle-class teachers' and 'working-class pupils'. In observations in a Welsh mining valley which still retained grammar and secondary modern schools, David Reynolds[25] found that good order reigned in the grammar schools because the pupils were committed to the same educational programme as the teachers on their behalf (mainly the pursuit of high status occupations). But in most of the secondary moderns, despite great differences in outlook, conflict was far less than might have been expected. This was because of a series of unofficial truces – the teachers would 'go easy' on the pupils and the pupils 'go easy' on the teachers. But in schools where there was no truce, class conflict was played out with dire results.

To liberals, an unspoken truce may seem entirely sensible (and something of this sort certainly appeared to be in operation in the English department at Abbey Wood). But the mere idea may be alarming both to traditional teachers and to many middle-class parents since it suggests that schools may 'buy' peace by identifying with working-class attitudes and abandoning the pursuit of 'high culture' and 'correct' behaviour. Some theorists writing from a Marxist position go further, apparently welcoming hostility to teachers as evidence of working-class 'resistance';[26] and this may fairly be regarded by conservatives as a genuine threat.

The whole question of Marxism or neo-Marxism in education has become increasingly important over the past few years. The period has seen the rise of the de-schoolers who argue, sometimes very plausibly, that the main effect of school is to indoctrinate children with the capitalist values of society. Left-wing teachers have also managed to create a good deal of panic over their intentions inside school. This springs from the assumption that some of them may be pledged to the destruction of institutions from within. Rank and File, a dissident, far-left grouping within the N.U.T., was sufficiently conspicuous in the early 1970s, despite a membership of not much more than 1000 in a profession of 500,000,[27] to be a target of sustained attack by mainline union leaders. Rank and File split up in 1976 and has not since re-emerged in any very impressive form. Nevertheless, anxiety about left-wing teachers still persists as a shaping force in public attitudes, and was given a powerful boost by the events at and surrounding William Tyndale school in 1975 and 1976.

Readers will remember that this was a junior school in Islington, in the Inner London Education Authority, which fell apart more publicly than any junior school had ever done before. Parents withdrew their children; the managers attempted to intervene; the I.L.E.A. tried to inspect; seven of the teachers went on strike, then set up their own school claiming they were victims of politicial victimization; a semi-judicial inquiry into these events went on for four months and ended with the dissident teachers, the managers, one leading Labour member of the I.L.E.A., the I.L.E.A. inspectorate and some officials all discredited in about equal parts. The managers resigned. So, after some prevarication, did Harvey Hinds, Labour chairman of the responsible I.L.E.A. committee. In 1978, after many more months of disciplinary hearings and appeal, Terry Ellis, the head, Brian Haddow, the leading Tyndale theorist, and three other teachers were finally dismissed. The implications for the system, in terms of school management, and local authority control, have proved to be enormous. In terms of public opinion, however, it was undoubtedly the educational politics of William Tyndale which mattered most.

It should be said at once that Terry Ellis, and all but one of the six members of staff who ranged themselves with him in this extraordinary dispute, have strenuously denied their membership of any political party or radical grouping. The only exception is Dorothy McColgan, a maths specialist who belonged to Rank and File.

Nevertheless, it is quite clear from the teachers' own account of their ideological position[28] that they were committed to teaching methods aimed at transforming, rather than endorsing, the structure of society. Their analysis opened with the statement that 'all education theories have a political basis'. They went on to illustrate this by the assertion that Black Paper theory 'demands that education be the tool that reinvigorates western capitalism and creates a society based on authoritarianism, élitism, a leadership principle, and the competition of man against man. It is a dynamic creed masquerading as an attempt to preserve the established order.' As for 'progressive education', that is often nothing but 'traditional education in disguise'. Modern-style teachers 'have been led, for instance, into claims that their methods achieve what formal education sets out to do, only better and for more children. In such a school unashamed coercion is no longer fashionable. Manipulation, more suited to indirect methods, has been substituted. Sir, as normal, is winning, and the children are still in their proper place, under firm control!' (The reference here is to schools like Prior Weston.)

Since the teachers' personal politics were a matter of contention, they refrained from spelling out the political implications of what they themselves were trying to do. But their programme clearly aimed at a different goal from the one that they ascribed to the Black Papers. It was school itself, they said, which by its compulsory nature and its conventions fractured 'any real personal contact between teachers and children'. (This was not very far from the position of the de-schoolers.) Tyndale teachers, they wrote of themselves, following a 'democratic, egalitarian and non-sexist philosophy', rejecting 'arbitrary standards of attainment and behaviour', encouraging children to ask questions rather than conditioning them to obey orders, 'sought to diminish the role-difference between them and their children, to a point where each could be seen to have something of value to offer the other on an equal level'. Education was not seen as 'a process of producing young people to fit into convenient niches'; children were encouraged to 'make their own decisions about their learning and lives'; the needs of those suffering from 'inner-city stress' were a priority.

The upshot of this highly idealistic doctrine was that children who would normally have gone to specialized schools because of behaviour problems were kept on in William Tyndale. The teachers were perhaps not well fitted to cope; certainly the behaviour problems were serious and affected many children. Large parts of the day were given over to a series of free options. 'Instead of becoming "self-motivated" by the new atmosphere of freedom pervading the Junior School', said the report of the Tyndale Inquiry,[29] 'the children became bored and listless.' Parents who wanted more structure for their children were denounced by Mr Ellis, so the inquiry heard in evidence, as 'working-class fascists or middle-class trendies out for their own children'.

Here in a nutshell was all that anyone had ever dreaded about progressive practice. And regardless of the practice, the theory itself was a frontal challenge not just to Cox and Boyson, or to Norman St John-Stevas, the Conservative shadow minister, but also to every fibre of the traditional, grammar-school-oriented, learning-motivated, social-democratic majority of the Labour Party.

And now, while the Tyndale volcano was still emitting brilliant sparks, another event took place which appeared to confirm the growing belief that matters were, if not precisely out of hand, at least in a highly parlous state. This was the publication in the spring of 1976 of a study of formal and informal teaching methods by Neville Bennett of Lancaster University.[30]

Dr Bennett took thirty-seven teachers whose methods ranged from highly formal to highly informal. He and his colleagues watched what happened in the classroom and examined the academic progress of the pupils, aged from ten to twelve-and-a-half. The results were startling; in a single school year the formally taught children shot ahead by three to four months in reading age, by three to four months in English and by four to five months in mathematics. Classroom observation showed, as the liberal-minded Professor Jerome Bruner of Oxford University summarized it in *New Society*, that 'the more formal the teaching, the more time pupils spend working on the subject matter at hand. And in general – though with some important exceptions – the more time pupils spend working on a subject, the more they improve at it . . .'[31] The study seemed a vindication of all that the traditionalists had been saying for almost a decade.

There were, however, grave complications. The single most successful teacher had used informal methods, though of a clearly organized and carefully structured kind. Press inquiries revealed that she was also highly experienced. Little account had been taken in the study of the level of experience of the teachers, though it may well have been that the traditional were in fact the more experienced. No account was taken of their individual quality, identified long ago in the Plowden Report as the 'most important' variable inside the school. Other factors which might have been even more important were also ignored. These included the home background of the children and the attitude of their parents. Major technical criticisms were made by liberal statisticians. Most unfortunate of all, perhaps, was the fact that though Bennett had begun with various gradations between formal and informal (so as to avoid the normal over-simplification), he lumped them together into just three categories – formal, informal and mixed – when he came to write up his results. This meant that one of the main effects of his study was to polarize the debate still further.

On any rational analysis, the Bennett study and the controversy which followed it demonstrated mainly that it is very hard in education to be sure about anything – not, as we have seen, that facts are particularly important anyway. The difficulties pointed out by the critics allowed the liberals to continue in their old beliefs, confident that nothing catastrophic had occurred. But traditionalists took it as a complete endorsement of their position. In terms of bringing on the Great Debate, it was at least among the final straws.

Notes

1. Cox, C. B., 'The Editing of *Critical Quarterly*', in *From Parnassus: Essays in Honor of Jacques Barzun*, ed. Weiner, Dora B., and Keylor, William R. (Harper and Row, 1976).
2. Cox, C. B., 'The Editing of *Critical Quarterly*', in *From Parnassus: Essays in Honor of Jacques Barzun*, ed. Weiner, Dora B., and Keylor, William R. (Harper and Row, 1976).
3. Cox, C. .B., 'Academic Freedom', in *University Independence*, ed. MacCallum Scott, John H. (Rex Collings, 1971).
4. Cox, C. B., and Dyson, A. E., (eds), *Fight for Education, a Black Paper* (and popularly known as 'the first Black Paper') (The Critical Quarterly Society, 1969).
5. Cox, C. B., and Dyson, A. E., (eds), *Black Paper Two* (The Critical Quarterly Society, 1969).
6. Cox, C. B., and Dyson, A. E., (eds), *Black Paper Three* (The Critical Quarterly Society, 1970).
7. Cox, C. B., and Boyson, Rhodes (eds), *Black Paper 1975* (J. M. Dent and Sons, 1975).
8. Cox, C. B., and Boyson, Rhodes (eds), *Black Paper 1977* (Temple Smith, 1977).
9. The main reason for resistance to national testing is the belief that it may have a restrictive effect in the classroom, with teachers teaching just to meet test requirements. The arguments are examined in 'Standards', Chapter Four.
10. Blackie, John, *Inside the Primary School* (H.M.S.O., 1967).
11. Wright, Nigel, *Progress in Education* (Croom Helm, 1977).

12. A member of Her Majesty's Inspectorate.
13. Interview with author.
14. The National Association of Schoolmasters/Union of Women Teachers. The two bodies amalgamated in 1976.
15. Start, K. B., and Wells, B. K., *The Trend of Reading Standards* (National Foundation for Educational research, 1972).
16. Morris, Dr Joyce, *Reading in the Primary School* (Newnes, 1959).
17. Horton, T. R., *The Reading Standards of Children in Wales* (National Foundation for Research in Education, 1973).
18. See, for example, Marland, Michael, *Language across the Curriculum* (Heinemann, 1977).
19. *Violent and Disruptive Behaviour in Schools* (N.A.S., 1975).
20. Boyson, Rhodes, *The Crisis in Education* (Woburn Press, 1975).
21. 'Disruptive Pupils', Education Officer's report to the Schools Sub-Committee, 20 January 1978.
22. Fogelman, Ken (ed.), *Britain's Sixteen Year-olds* (National Children's Bureau, 1976).
23. The National Child Development Study appears to have lost the remaining 1 per cent.
24. Stone, Judith, and Taylor, Felicity, *Vandalism in Schools* (The Save the Children Fund, 1977).
25. In *Working Together for Children and Their Families* (Welsh Office, 1977).
26. See 'Social Democracy, Education and the Crisis', by Dann Finn, Neil Grant and Richard Johnson in *Cultural Studies* 10, 1977 (University of Birmingham).
27. Wright, Nigel, *Progress in Education* (Croom Helm, 1977). The teaching profession as a whole is discussed below in 'The Teachers', Chapter Four.
28. See Chapter Four of *William Tyndale: The Teachers' Story*, by Terry Ellis, Jackie McWhirter, Dorothy McDolgan and Brian Haddow (Writers and Readers Publishing Cooperative, 1976).
29. Auld, Q. C., Robin, *William Tyndale Junior and Infants School Public Inquiry* I.L.E.A., 1976).
30. Bennet, Neville, *Teaching Styles and Pupil Progress* (Open Books, 1976).
31. 26 April 1976.

4. Problems on the public agenda

I: Launching the Great Debate

When James Callaghan became prime minister in the spring of 1976, he seems to have been well aware that education, even if no great concern of his own, was fast acquiring the status of a major problem. This was an issue on which Labour could lose a lot of votes unless a convincing initiative were taken. Education also raised, in the sharpest possible form, the question of value for money at a time of economic crisis. Despite cuts in planned increases for future spending, even some cuts in the substance of education itself, the service was still mopping up between £6 and £7 billion a year. Yet what was there to show for it? Nothing much, it might have seemed, apart from bitter controversy over standards and almost total lack of progress in bringing working-class children into better jobs or higher education. This had always been one of Labour's foremost aims but now it appeared that as fast as places in higher education were increased, middle-class youngsters came forward to occupy them. In 1970, 44 per cent of new students in university, polytechnic and college were children of professional people, administrators or managers, even though these represented only about a quarter of the total population. By 1975 this had risen to 51 per cent.[1] Middle-class Richmond was sending 17 per cent of the appropriate age group to university, the east London borough of Barking only 2·4 per cent. This was not what the Labour party meant by equality of opportunity. Mr Callaghan called in Fred Mulley, then the education secretary, and the two men talked for a long time. As a result, the Department of Education and Science was asked to draw up a memorandum on the four problems that seemed most critical: the teaching of the 'three Rs' in primary school; the question of what older children should study in comprehensives; the examination system; and the general problem of sixteen- to nineteen-year-olds who had no prospect of going on directly to higher education. This last issue seemed, and still remains, enormously important. Great numbers were out of work and industrialists were suggesting that many of them were unfitted for any kind of job because of low standards in reading, writing and mathematics. The plan was for Mr Callaghan to use the memorandum as the basis for a speech, or series of speeches, in the autumn.

In the event, the briefing paper did a lot of his work for him. It was written largely by Her Majesty's Inspectorate, a body housed within the Department of Education and Science but theoretically independent and thus immune from political pressures. Yet when the memorandum became public that September, having been leaked to the *Guardian*, it was evident that the Inspectorate were responding to many of the same anxieties as Mr Callaghan and the public. This document, known as the Yellow Paper because of its somewhat jaundiced covers, contained little to cheer the reader. Plowdenesque teaching methods, though fully adopted in only a minority of schools, had had a widespread effect on primary schools, the Yellow Paper said, and while in able hands they produced relaxed, confident and happy children, they could prove a trap to less-able and less-experienced teachers. 'The challenge now is to restore the rigour without damaging the real benefits of child-centred development.' In secondary schools, many weaknesses were diagnosed. The 'more participatory style' of modern schools could allow pupils to choose unbalanced or not particularly profitable courses of study or to opt 'in numbers insufficient for the country's needs for scientific and technological subjects'. The current concentration on preparing the young for their roles in society may have led to a corresponding under-concentration on preparing them for their economic role.

The teaching force, because of its recent and rapid expansion, contained a disproportionate number of young and inexperienced teachers and, said the Yellow Paper, in one of its most damning phrases, 'the average is probably below what used to be expected in, for example, a good grammar school'. Teachers needed plenty of in-service training. On the question of who should study what, a solution to some of the problems might lie in trying to establish 'generally accepted principles for the composition of the secondary curriculum for all pupils, that is to say a "core curriculum" '.

All this, of course, was inflammatory stuff. A careless reading of the words suggested not just a major traditionalist backlash in the Inspectorate but also that the state might be on the brink of imposing a centralized curriculum, something that had always been dreaded by people in education, and all the more so since the fearful successes of a state-imposed curriculum in Nazi Germany. Few paused to reflect that the wording over primary schools left some room at least for a defence of modern methods and that what was proposed for the curriculum was a set of 'generally accepted principles' – a phrase which could mean everything or nothing. Uproar broke out in the educational world.

The section of the Yellow Paper dealing with sixteen- to nineteen-year-olds and the relationship of schools to the economy caused less immediate anguish. The problems were plain to see and it seemed reasonable to wonder, as the Yellow Paper did, whether enough material of 'vocational relevance' was provided for fourteen- and fifteen-year-olds. But the section on exams proved almost as inflammatory as that on the core curriculum.

To explain what was happening, it is necessary to go back a little. The C.S.E. exam, discussed in previous chapters, was introduced in 1965 as a result of the government-sponsored Beloe Report in 1960. In the intervening period a new body was set up to 'advise' the government on exams and the curriculum. This was the Schools Council. It had a majority of teacher-union representatives on all its committees and it took teacher power very seriously indeed. R. H. Tawney had written long ago that 'the aim should be to make our educational system an organic unity, alive in every part, served by teachers united, self-govern-

ing and free'.[2] This, or something close to it, was the credo of
the Schools Council. It meant that the Schools Council
identified itself with the C.S.E. approach.

The powers of the Schools Council were always limited by
the fact that the Secretary of State was under no obligation to
take its advice; and, in fact, Mrs Thatcher in 1972 threw out a
Schools Council recommendation to change the grading system
at 'A' level. Nevertheless, from 1970 onwards the Council was
very much occupied with its proposals for a new exam at sixteen-plus to replace 'O' level and C.S.E.; and these seemed to
imply the most radical extension yet of teacher-power, with a
heavy reliance on the Mode III principle. Considerable research
was conducted by the Schools Council into possibilities for an
exam of this kind and by 1976 the proposals were ready. It was,
however, clear to all who scrutinized them that there still remained a good deal of confusion over the administration of the
exams (mainly because of differences of opinion between the
school-centred C.S.E. boards and the more university-centred
approach of the G.C.E. boards). Much of the research had been
into the possibilities of an exam that could be common to all.
This had been abandoned in favour of proposals for a common system. But the common system itself remained under-
researched, and open to the criticism that while the most able
might not be fully stretched, the least able would be somewhat
confused. When the main decision-making body of the Schools
Council debated the proposals, the universities, the G.C.E.
boards and the independent schools were heavily opposed. But
the teacher unions were, of course, in favour. And so, because
of the composition of the Schools Council, the sixteen-plus proposals were accepted and forwarded to the Secretary of State
for Education. This was a major defeat for the universities and
all who identified themselves with university values, and it appeared to many observers to be a naked bid for power by the
teachers.

In response to this, the Yellow Paper pointed out all the
obvious difficulties in the sixteen-plus proposals and simultaneously launched a fierce attack on the Schools Council. De-

spite some 'good quality staff work', its performance on examinations and the curriculum had been generally mediocre. Moreover, it said, 'the influence of the teacher unions has led to an increasingly political flavour – in the worst sense of the word – in its deliberations'. The general reputation of the Schools Council had 'suffered a considerable decline over the last few years'. The Yellow Paper proposed a new constitution for the Council, and a leading role for the D.E.S. and the Inspectorate in the development of education. The prime minister, the Yellow Paper said, 'would have to respect legitimate claims made by the teachers as to the exercise of their professional judgment, but should firmly refute any argument – and this is what they have sought to establish – that no one except teachers has any right to any say in what goes on in schools'. Partly because of the Schools Council's injudicious exam proposals, teacher power was one of the main targets the Yellow Paper shot at.

As far as the Schools Council was concerned, the timing of the onslaught was unfortunate, for its chairman, Sir Alex Smith, head of Manchester Polytechnic and one of the most level-headed men in education, had already been moving privately towards achieving a new and more realistic balance in its constitution. Now he felt personally betrayed. And in respect of a Yellow Paper assertion that the Inspectorate is 'without doubt the most powerful single agency to influence what goes on in schools, both in kind and standard', Sir Alex asked whether it was not the Inspectorate rather than the Schools Council which should take the blame if matters were in a mess.

By the time that Mr Callaghan came to make his speech on education at Ruskin College in Oxford, a centre for Labour and trades union education, there was already a semi-official recognition that education in school was in some difficulty; and government and teachers were potentially at loggerheads.

Mr Callaghan walked warily, claiming a right for public discussion while trying to avoid a complete break with the teachers. In a speech of trenchant commonplaces he nevertheless managed to touch on most of the points that bothered most people. Unwilling to allow that twenty years of Labour-inspired reform might have been pushing in the wrong direction, he declared that he was not one of those who would paint 'a lurid picture of educational decline because I do not believe it is generally true'. But he conceded that there were 'examples which give cause for concern' (the William Tyndale affair had reached one of its early apogees the previous month) and drew attention, along Yellow Paper lines, to worries over informal teaching methods in primary schools, unbalanced curricula in secondary schools and to the proposed exam reform which he delivered firmly into the hands of Shirley Williams. (She had recently been appointed Education Secretary, presumably in an attempt to bring a little more charm into a contentious area and because she might also be expected to create an impression of urgency.) But the point which Mr Callaghan developed most sharply was the basic gap between industry and our educational system. 'I have been concerned', he said, 'to find that many of our best trained students who have completed the higher levels of education at university or polytechnic have no desire to join industry . . . there seems to be a need for a more technological bias in science teaching that will lead towards practical applications in industry rather than towards academic studies.'

Because of the advance publicity, Mr Callaghan's speech became a major 'media event' and it was this as much as its content which made it so important. No new policies were proposed, but the government had now established that educational standards, and the relationship of education to the economy, were to be as much of a priority as comprehensive reform in isolation.

In his speech, Mr Callaghan called for a Great Debate. The next step was a series of nine regional conferences. They were to be attended by teachers, parents, industrialists and educational administrators and were to cover four main themes, pulled together from the Yellow Paper and Mr Callaghan's speech. These were: the curriculum; standards and their assessment; the education and training of teachers; and school and working life. A fifth and equally vital theme – the question of who should control the schools – was omitted as it was being covered, in part, by the Taylor Committee's investigation into governors and managers.[3]

The nine conferences turned out, as bitterly predicted by the N.U.T., to consist mainly of the delivery at two-minute intervals of an inordinate number of prepared statements of well-known positions. Some of the key speeches were interesting. So was the enmity to be observed between the teachers and the industrialists and in some cases between the teachers and the parents. Supporting papers also produced evidence of one or two shifts in the policies of the participants. But the main result of the conferences was to provide a text of every kind on every theme – the government later picked out the ones that favoured its own policies – and to stimulate an enormous amount of lay discussions both privately and, in particular, on television. In this way, something approaching a Great Debate really did take place in 1977.

In the rest of this chapter I shall take the five main themes in turn, in each case trying to sketch in enough of the background to make the issues comprehensible. This, I hope, will enable the reader to understand the implications behind the policy decisions already taken (and reviewed in the final chapter of this book) and behind those which may be taken in the years to come.

II: Curriculum and teaching method

What should children learn, and how should they be taught?

Though the regional conferences allowed no serious place for discussion of teaching method, it is impossible to separate the question of what children should learn from that of how it should be taught. In terms of progressive primary schools, the reason is a simple one. The actual methods of learning and the way the children are treated are consciously seen as under-pinning all the other aims of the teachers. They are part of the purpose of education. This was made clear by the Plowden Report:

> A school is not merely a teaching shop, it must transmit values and attitudes. It is a community in which children learn to live first and foremost as children and not as future adults. The school sets out deliberately to devise the right environment for children, to allow them to be themselves and to develop in the way and at the pace appropriate to them.

In more formal primary schools, in which there is less stress on the importance of the present and more stress on the future value of what is being learned, it is also undoubtedly the case – though this is less often consciously realized and far less frequently expressed – that the more hierarchical structure is a preparation for a society whose hierarchies are well respected by the teachers. In both cases, method and content are inseparable; and since it is modern teaching methods which have caused so much anxiety, an evaluation of the curriculum must take into account the success or failure of these methods. In secondary schools, too, widely differing attitudes to education are embodied in differing approaches to the curriculum; and here it is the success or failure of mixed-ability teaching which must come under scrutiny. In the following pages I shall look at primary and secondary education separately, starting in each case with teaching method and then moving on to other curricular issues. The aim is not to advance any thesis but to identify genuine problems, eliminate the spurious ones, and illuminate, if possible, some of the solutions that have been suggested. In considering the secondary curriculum, this will involve a discussion of the rival philosophies underlying both the idea of the common core and opposition to it.

Primary Method

So far as primary schools are concerned, there is no convincing evidence that traditional methods are better than modern, or, indeed, vice versa. The trouble here is that educational research is so complicated that it is almost always possible to find fault with the results of any piece of work. The Bennett study described in the last chapter is a case in point. Here was a substantial and careful inquiry, conducted without any obvious bias on the part of the researchers, under the most respectable of academic auspices, and making every attempt to avoid the errors of past research. Yet in the event it proved wide open to criticism because it had neglected important variables. It seems that there are so many variables in dealing with children that it is beyond human ingenuity to cater for all of them at once. As Nigel Wright suggests in *Progress in Education*, the best one can do is register the shortcomings of each piece of work, and try to fit the existing pieces together jig-saw fashion. In this way, the Bennett study emerges as just one in a somewhat contradictory series of British research findings, whose main purport is that there is not much discernible difference in achievement between children taught by formal or informal methods.[4] This has received confirmation in a recent study in America which surveyed the performance of 30,000 children in eighty, supposedly representative, schools, and concluded that such innovations as team teaching, open classrooms, movable timetables and individualized instruction made precious little difference to results. In Britain, at least, home background seems more likely to determine results than anything that happens at school. As for school itself, the most important factor is probably the skill and experience of the teacher. If Bennett can be said to have proved anything specific,[5] it is that teachers who follow a coherent and carefully planned approach, whether formal or informal and just as recommended by Professor Bantock in Black Paper Two, are likely to do better by their children in terms of academic achievement than those who let them slop around in what one writer has described as 'an endless wet playtime'.

In the educational debate of 1977, however, the question was how many teachers had abdicated control, either from conviction, from inexperience or from laziness. Here the Inspectorate were better placed than anybody to make a judgement;

and the Yellow Paper, as we have seen, showed serious worry over younger and less-able teachers. This was because they often failed to realize the importance of a systematic approach, involving not just the careful planning of teaching opportunities but also close attention to the performance and progress of each individual child. Evidence which H.M.I.s were at that time collecting as part of systematic survey of primary schools suggested that while teachers had some idea of the level of performance to expect when children joined primary school and when they left it, they were very vague about what to expect in between. Lack of clarity about ways in which children made progress could be a barrier to planned progression in teaching. Meanwhile it was revealed both at the William Tyndale inquiry and through the rumpus in Tameside, that, in some junior schools at least, proper records on the achievement of individual children were not being kept. This was an obvious threat to any real continuity, either between class and class or between school and school. In general, there seemed to be a good deal of inefficiency about; and the effects were particularly grave in schools which failed to demand a structured approach from teachers. The reason did not lie in modern methods but in their sloppy application.

That this situation should have arisen was deeply regrettable, not least because the possibility had been foreseen from the beginning by some of the most gifted of informal teachers. Here, for example, is Sybil Marshall, a former village headteacher, writing in 1963,[6] four years *before* the Plowden Report. If traditional methods returned, she said, it would not be on account of the traditionalists but because of 'those greater enemies of real modern education, the people who embrace anarchy in the name of freedom . . .':

Let no young teacher reading this get any false ideas from it. To control a class in freedom, to learn with each child instead of instructing a passive class, to be a well of clear water into which the children can dip all the time, instead of a hosepipe dousing them with facts, is the most exhausting way of all of doing a teacher's job.

One explanation for the fact that some teachers failed to

learn this, may lie in the enormous expansion of the primary teaching force in the late 1960s and early 1970s. Naturally enough, most of the teachers were young and had not yet learned through experience how much would be demanded of them. Today, however, the number of children in primary schools is dropping quickly. Far fewer new teachers will be entering the service for a decade or two to come. The existing teacher force will therefore be a large proportion of the teaching force we have; and they, of necessity, will become more experienced. Even in 1976, when Mr Callaghan spoke, there seemed some chance that a spontaneous cure might already be taking place.

Another major factor had been the rapid turnover of teachers in the late 1960s and early 1970s, above all in the cities (in London in 1973 it was 25 per cent). This was probably far more serious in terms of resulting discontinuity and lack of firm control than any misunderstandings of modern teaching method. But again, because of the falling school rolls, the number of vacant jobs into which existing teachers can move is far smaller today and so this problem too will be diminishing.

For these two reasons it is arguable that the public reaction against informal methods, found at its crudest in popular newspapers and dignified by Mr Callaghan in his Ruskin speech, occurred somewhat *after* the real crisis in schools and at a moment when things were getting better. The time was almost certainly ripe, the Yellow Paper said, for 'a corrective shift of emphasis'. But a swing was already occurring on its own, and it seemed that the extra propulsion given by the Great Debate might push it right out of control.

One immediate response – and unequivocally a good one – was an enormous improvement in record-keeping in primary schools. Headteachers, having seen colleagues exposed, rushed to repair their dress. But the most unfortunate consequence has been that in many schools, the 'basics' of maths (the four rules, of addition, subtraction, division and multiplication), along with grammar, spelling and punctuation have now been separated out from the rest of the curriculum and made the subject of a great deal of mechanical drilling.

Sheila Browne, Her Majesty's Senior Chief Inspector – that is to say, the head of the Inspectorate – noted with evident regret in a major speech in July 1977[7] that the swing towards the basic skills was allowing them to become separated from their application. A month later, in another important speech,[8] Norman Thomas, the Chief Inspector for Primary Education, spoke of indications that reading drills had become unduly emphasized recently in some schools – 'perhaps in an unthinking reaction to public disquiet about reading standards or from reading press reports rather than Dr Bennett's own words'. Virginia Makins in her *Times Educational Supplement* articles[9] said that where this occurred the overwhelming impression was one of dullness.

The truth of the matter was that in the Yellow Paper, and in the government Green Paper which followed in July 1977, repeating many of the main themes concerning primary education, officialdom itself helped to stampede the schools into over-reaction. The Inspectors now found themselves obliged to use all the room they had allowed themselves in the Yellow Paper to try to counteract the unfortunate effects of their own preaching. The very essentials of the modern method stood at risk.

Primary Curriculum

Of the content of the primary syllabus, less need be said. Contrary to myth, there is no great variation from school to school or area to area.[10] Almost without exception the main priority is given to 'language skills' – reading, writing and the spoken word. Then comes mathematics, with the four rules taking precedence over investigation and practical work. (There may be great variation in the approach, however. There is room for a good deal of tidying up, together with more awareness of priorities.) Then follow such social and personal studies as history, geography and religious education; and art, craft and music. These latter 'aesthetic subjects' have been set at risk by the back-to-basics movement; and this, as much as drills divorced from application, is an evident denial of the main aims of modern teaching method. French exists now only tenuously in primary schools, a great expansion in the 1960s having proved generally disastrous – though more because of the quality of teaching than any inherent difficulty in the language itself.

Science, too, is taught less than might be expected, given its obvious suitability for discovery learning. There are some signs, though, that simple scientific ideas will be introduced more frequently in years to come.

Secondary Teaching Method

'Streaming' is a relatively recent invention, developed as a liberal response to the idea that intelligence is innate and that each child has an immutable ceiling of ability. If this were so, what more appropriate than specialized teaching for groups made up of children whose ability was about the same? In the post-war years, however, as the 'environmentalists' came into their own, asserting that home background and social circumstances were of great importance in determining a child's level of performance, confidence in segregation began to collapse. Ability, it now seemed, was variable in time and variable between one subject and another. The result was the (limited) swing towards mixed-ability grouping described in Chapter Two.

This happened first in primary schools as the disappearance of selection at eleven began to remove competitive pressure. Since that time, in areas where selection has finally gone, the primary schools have often been criticized because of innovations such as discovery learning. But mixed-ability teaching itself has scarcely attracted any controversy. In many secondary schools, however, it is *the* burning issue.

The weight of the evidence contradicts the conservatives' belief that mixed-ability teaching is disastrous. Overall, in academic terms, it seems that the actual form of organization does not count for very much. In social terms, however, mixed ability may bring some gains.

In Britain, this picture of social gain and academic unimportance first emerged from a substantial and widely respected, though frequently misrepresented, study of primary schools.[11] It has been given credibility by research in the U.S.A. In terms of the early years of British *secondary* schooling (the years when mixed-ability teaching is most common) the Barker Lunn picture received convincing confirmation in 1977 with the publication of results of an inquiry[12] at Banbury in Oxfordshire. In this project, two of four 'halls' at Banbury School were taught in streamed classes for their first two years, two in mixed-ability groups. Some 2000 pupils and several intakes were covered by the study. The general objectives were the same throughout the school. The children were tested in English, maths, science and French. In most tests there was nothing to choose between the streamed and unstreamed halls. Mixed-ability pupils did better in free writing. In biology and French, where the streamed pupils scored more, this seemed to be due to particularly successful individual teachers. Academic achievement was more closely related to such factors as the primary school the child had previously attended and the skill, experience and reputation of teachers, than it was to streaming or unstreaming. But in terms of attitude, it seemed that there was greater satisfaction with the school among pupils in the unstreamed classes, particularly when compared with those in lower streams in the other halls. There was also greater social integration. Children in the unstreamed classes were more likely to make friends with children of different ability or different social class.

Dr David Newbold, the author of the report, concluded that since the academic differences were negligible 'other considerations, and this may mean largely social, can be pre-eminent in the planning of the lower secondary school'.

Against this is the undisputed fact that mixed-ability teaching is much more work. When properly applied, it requires the teacher to prepare what may amount to individual lessons for many individual children and the process of getting round to everybody in the class may be physically and emotionally exhausting. Assessment and record keeping are also much harder.

Many experts, like Lord Alexander,[13] secretary of the Association of Education Committees (until its dismemberment in 1977), believe that only the most gifted teachers can engage successfully in mixed-ability teaching. But this idea, though fast becoming part of the conventional wisdom, has been challenged recently in a Schools Council survey of mixed-ability teaching in mathematics.[14] 'In the departments we have seen', said the report, 'there was plenty of evidence that, given good departmental organization and a supportive head of department, many teachers who would be modest about their individual capacities have tackled the new problems with success.' On this point judgement must be suspended.

In summary, though, it seems that Charles Stuart-Jervis, head of Abbey Wood, is right – teachers may be expected to make the greatest success of the method they believe in. Mixed-ability teaching is hard work for every teacher and, as Mr Stuart-Jervis adds, it is disproportionately hard work for the inexperienced. It follows, therefore, to use the words of Margaret Reid, principal officer of an N.F.E.R. inquiry into mixed-ability teaching, that the question of whether or not to organize like this 'can only be approached by each school appraising its beliefs, defining its objectives and considering how these are likely to be achieved in its own special circumstances – circumstances in which staffing facilities, pupil intake and the expectations of the surrounding community may be of paramount importance'.[15]

This is the picture presented by academic research. A rather more worrying picture has been built up during the period of the Great Debate – and largely by Her Majesty's Inspectorate. An H.M.I. report[16] suggested that where mixed-ability teaching took place in modern languages it was accentuating the difficulties already experienced in schools. Unity was being achieved at the expense of quality, said the report.

The most able pupils remained unchallenged, and if the average and below-average were not actually discouraged, neither were they in any way inspired. The need to cater for a wide ability-range in every teaching group . . . was producing a very low common denominator of language achievement.

In a paper on mathematics, drawn up as background for participants in the regional conferences (which ignored the whole question of mixed ability), the inspectors said it produced a climate in which expectations were too low, reliance on worksheets excessive and the use of language devalued.[17] All these objections were drawn together for a major conference on comprehensives at York in December 1977, where, in a paper on school organization,[18] the Inspector authors complained that many teachers of mixed-ability classes were still using traditional, whole-group methods and pitching their lessons 'at some estimate of the "middle" with almost certain failure to satisfy either extreme'. Many others had virtually abandoned 'teaching', yet the cards and worksheets they were using for individualized learning were 'not always of adequate quality'.

These statements, though resting on assertion rather than on quantified analysis, are the result of direct, classroom observation by experienced men and women. They have to be taken seriously. Their net result, however, appears to have been some loss of confidence in the mixed-ability teaching rather than – the other possibility – a determination to do it better.

A second attack on mixed-ability teaching is also developing along political lines. Some Conservative authorities, particularly in rural areas, have become distinctly hostile to it. This is related to the 'equality of opportunity' argument.

Traditional schools often assert, and sometimes very plausibly, that they are providing equal opportunity for all children *to have their differing needs catered for*. Most supporters of mixed-ability teaching believe that they are doing the same, mainly by individualized learning and in a framework that favours social integration, Banbury-style, and social cooperation. This is a very common position among mainline Labour teachers and is consistent with our normal social-democratic approach and the needs of a mixed economy. It assumes that children will ultimately take their place in society, with all its existing hierarchies and 'class places' and that change should be gradual, a matter of reform rather than revolution. The adoption of mixed-ability teaching on these grounds should theoretically be acceptable to Conservatives. But there is also a small number of teachers on the left of the Labour party and to their left again who believe that one of the aims of education is to eliminate differences between children. What seems to be happening is that Conservatives equate this kind of egalitarianism, rare though it is, with mixed-ability teaching in general. This seems a particularly unfortunate misunderstanding. Even inside the mainline Labour party there are signs of growing doubt about mixed-ability teaching. These provide a measure of the extent to which the grammar-wing is asserting itself over the egalitarians.

Mixed-ability teaching is thus controversial both academically and politically. But on one important issue, the education of gifted children, it deserves no special blame. An H.M.I. report concluded that our brightest children – the ablest 2 per cent or so – were just as likely to be neglected in streamed as in unstreamed schools.[19]

The Secondary Curriculum

The critical question opened up by Mr Callaghan and the Yellow Paper was the possibility of a common-core curriculum. Mr Callaghan clearly had it in mind to cure the nation's ills by adjusting the content of education. But before anything of the kind may be attempted in a democracy it is necessary to ask such basic questions as whether the personal goals of the individual can be identified with the needs of society. Is society merely the sum of its disparate parts, whatever those may be? Or is there some general goal to which the individual should be subordinated?

Mr Callaghan, in his Ruskin speech, declared in his bluff and simple-seeming way that there was no conflict between the individual and society. The goals of education were: 'to equip children to the best of their ability for a lively, constructive place in society and also to fit them for a job of work. Not one or the other, but both.' This reference to jobs of work and constructive places in society presupposes that both are available for all comers, an extremely dubious proposition which is explored later in this chapter in the section on 'School and Work'. In terms of the curriculum, however, it need only be said at this point that it was because Mr Callaghan held this belief and had a clear view of the best direction for society that he felt able to say with confidence how he thought children should be educated. His personal preference, he declared, was for a common core; and it was plain that he envisaged this as a minimum number of things that everyone should know.

Tim Devlin and Mary Warnock, in their joint book on the Great Debate[20] (intended both as a summary and a contribution) adopted this view and elaborated it in an interesting argument of which it is possible here to give only the main heads. Work, they wrote, was better than idleness, 'valuable for itself and not only for the monetary rewards it brings'. Certain clearly defined things must therefore be learned to equip a child to take an active, working place in industrial society. But the good life was also founded on a capacity for pleasure. In pursuit of this, schools should try to develop in pupils such skills and attributes as fluent reading, keen observation, active imagination. Another obligation was to meet the demands of higher education, so that learning at a more advanced level could continue after school. 'In meeting all these needs', wrote Devlin and Warnock, 'the school is preparing the pupil for one thing: independence' – but independence, quite explicitly, within the framework of existing society. A great many people, though not, presumably, the authors and their children – nor Mr Callaghan and his family – would on this analysis have to spend their lives in factory production lines.

Because it is specific about the goals of society, this kind of argument permits the construction of a core curriculum defined in terms of subjects; and most of the Devlin–Warnock volume is devoted to saying what these should be. But the argument is also frequently associated, as in Devlin and Warnock, with the idea that education is for the future, and is to be rated a success to the extent that it improves the future life of the pupil. This, of course, is different in emphasis from the Plowdenesque notion suggested on page 108, that the present counts as well as the future and that the quality of school life must be, to some considerable extent, its own justification.

If, in fact, one uses variation in attitude to present and future as a touchstone, grouping on one side those who attach real value to the present and on the other those whose educational aims are directed mainly towards the future, two broad, though overlapping tendencies begin to emerge. The full-frontal futurists tend to be more respectful of hierarchies. Paradoxically, they accept society much as it is today, or even long for a return to an idealized past. They believe in exams and competition, less for the good of children's souls than as a way of helping them through the bottlenecks of education (into higher education, for example) and later through the bottlenecks of adult life. They sometimes admire success regardless of its object. Above all, they subscribe to the ideal of the 'educated man', somebody whose youth has equipped him with most of the things it is appropriate to know – including a code of honour and behaviour. They therefore have no trouble in accepting a core curriculum.

But inherent in this approach there are two considerable risks. One is that the concept of the 'educated man' will be defined too narrowly, his education merely reflecting the views of one generation or one social class, with convergent thinkers preferred to divergent and originality undervalued. (Some feel that the public schools and university examining boards fall into this trap.) The other, closely related, risk is that because so much importance is attributed to the end product, the process of the child's development will be neglected.

The partial-futurists are distinguished from the full-futurists mainly by their interest in development and in all the diverse potentialities of the individual. As for the future, they want to produce good citizens for a world which would be improved by many changes. Inevitably these ideas imply a less rigid concept of education and a less authoritarian structure. And once one starts to think like this a subject-based common core begins to look less attractive.

Unfortunately, the curriculum is an area which lends itself to much abstract and windy philosophizing. In recent years, the partial-futurists have been struggling to find some kind of formula for acceptable diversity, that is to say a *pattern* or *framework* for a variable education in which, despite the variety, one may be certain that each individual will be encouraged to learn and develop in all the most important ways. Curiously enough, it is Her Majesty's Inspectorate who have come up with what appears to be potentially the most useful of the various frameworks proposed – and about the only one that is readily comprehensible.

The essence of this experimental framework is a list of the areas of experience and understanding considered essential for all pupils.[21] These, in alphabetical order, might run as follows: the aesthetic and creative, the ethical, the linguistic, the mathematical, the physical, the scientific, the social and political, the spiritual. If it were agreed that a substantial part of the curriculum should be devoted to these areas, then the 'magnificent eight' could be used as a check list for curriculum construction in the early years of secondary schooling; and in the later years, when choice was allowed, the guiding principle would be that nobody could opt out at any stage from any of these areas. This would not mean that the basic skills were ignored – indeed the one aim on which everybody agrees is that all pupils should be fully literate and numerate – but it would provide a framework for a well-balanced education over and above the common skills. The other essential point is that though this framework would allow for a liberal approach in a way that a minimum common core does *not*, it would also allow for the more hard-nosed approach of the futurists. It is easy to interpret, as Sheila Browne explained, in terms of a student's being enabled 'to interrelate with his environment, to take his place in society and in work, to be prepared for the matters of fundamental concern in adult life, and to be introduced to a selection of the essential elements of our complicated civilization and culture'. Accommodating liberal and traditional approaches to education, it would be a tool and not a master.

All this, however, is some time in the future. For the moment, effective discussion must be limited to the main subject areas. And as one begins to probe a little beneath the surface, it is easy to understand why lack of balance in the curriculum was one of the main concerns of the Great Debate.

Most schools, in the first two or three years, try to provide 'the maximum common experience'. (York conference paper.) A typical programme will include: English, mathematics, science, French, history, geography, religious education, art, craft, home economics, music and physical education. Some of these subjects may be grouped together, with, for example, English, history and geography combined to make a course of 'integrated studies' in the 'humanities'. (Integrated studies, which are often associated with mixed-ability teaching, have come under a lot of inspectorial criticism lately for lack of rigour and forethought. These criticisms lead, as with mixed ability, to two possible conclusions: either that they should be abandoned or that they should be done better. In my view, there is a lot to be said for the latter course.)

Even in the first, common years, however, a good deal of diversity creeps in. The least able, in order to help them acquire basic skills in which they are lacking, are often given special coaching, but not necessarily in such a way that success allows them to rejoin the mainstream option-pattern later on. 'You therefore have the strange situation that something which was intended to increase opportunities limits them significantly' (Sheila Browne). In grammar schools, catering for the more academic children, there is usually a chance to begin a classical or second foreign language in the early years. But in comprehensive schools, where there is greater emphasis on technological, craft and aesthetic subjects, demand for classics or a second language is often so low that these courses become totally uneconomic. 'Consequently there is a reduction in opportunity that was never intended – and a reduction important not just to the pupils' (Sheila Browne). Not only this – an H.M.I. survey published in 1975[22] found that an astonishing 28 per cent of secondary schools in England were affected by premature specialization in the first three years. The Inspectors also identified another pattern, described as 'pre-emptive', in which a pupil would not be allowed to take up a particular subject later unless he or she had studied some other specific subject as a prelude. (Thus, for example, only those who had previously taken metal work might be allowed to go on to technical drawing.) This affected 27 per cent of mixed-sex schools in England. (No figure is given for single-sex schools.)

This is bad enough, but from the age of about fourteen, when the recognized option-system starts, the difficulties multiply almost exponentially. The common core is now extremely small – most typically just English, maths, physical education and perhaps, as the law requires, a smattering of religious education. (The Inspectors behave as if R.E. was really taught; a recent survey by the Association of Assistant Masters suggested that it had disappeared in the majority of schools.)[23] Over half the timetable is now optional, consisting of perhaps an extra four or five subjects chosen from fifteen or twenty. And from now on, there is even sharper differentiation between the more and the less able. The latter usually have a limited choice, 'with a greater emphasis on craft subjects and on general courses bearing such labels as "social studies", "environmental studies" and "design for living" ' (York papers). Academically gifted children tend to end up, whatever the system of discussion and consultation in the school, with a heavily academic timetable in which the creative, aesthetic and practical side of their development is often almost totally ignored. (A clever girl, for instance, is most unlikely to learn anything about baby care or unit pricing.)

From this, they move on towards even greater specialization, culminating, most probably, in just two or three subjects offered at 'A' level. Because of this narrowly specialist approach at sixth-form level, students make such great progress that universities and polytechnics are generally able to run high-quality degree courses lasting three years, as opposed to the four-year courses common in other countries. But there is no doubt that premature specialization means loss of opportunities in later life. Accordingly, the Schools Council has been considering a change at sixth-form level. Under this scheme a student would take exams in five subjects, three at 'N' or 'normal' level and two at 'F' or 'further' level. The 'N' subjects would take half the study time that would have been given to an 'A' level, the 'F' subjects three-quarters. There 'N' and 'F' exams, discussed in more detail below, would entirely replace 'A' levels. But there seems some possibility that to go for breadth instead of depth, however desirable for the sixth-former himself, would make it necessary to extend university degree courses for four full years if standards were to be maintained. This, in turn, would involve enormous costs and radical changes in plan for university expansion. The proposal is thus extremely controversial.

The narrowing of choice through specialization at fourteen-plus is perhaps less spectacular than at sixth-form level, but it affects more people. During the Great Debate, particular worries were expressed over the number giving up maths, sciences and foreign languages, all of them subjects related to our economic success, at too early a stage. It is to these that I shall now turn.

The Inspectors found that, contrary to prevailing myth, maths occupied about one eighth of the secondary curriculum, and that very few people gave it up before sixteen. 'In sixteen-plus examinations and in the sixth form the numbers of pupils taking mathematics were second only to the numbers taking English.' There had been a 3·5 per cent increase in the number of boys passing 'A' level maths between 1964 and 1974 and a 30·3 per cent increase (from a very low base) in the number of girls. Since 1972, however, the increase had not been maintained at the same level, and this was beginning to cause worry. There were rather greater problems over continuity, maths being one of those 'linear' subjects in which one learns step by step as if ascending a ladder. Continuity between school and school was often almost nil, with progression sometimes poorly planned inside the schools themselves. The differences between school and school were also legion. University teachers might find themselves confronted by a group of first-year students who had followed any one of almost fifty syllabuses. This made teaching extremely difficult and here at least there seemed a case for agreeing on a common minimum.

The number of those giving up science was far more worrying. Figures for the first fifty schools examined in a major H.M.I. survey of secondary schools (due for publication in 1979), showed that in the fourth year, 6 per cent of boys and 13 per cent of girls did no science at all. In the fifth year, the number of boys held constant at 6 per cent. But the number of girls doing no science had jumped to 17 per cent. Moreover, although it is generally reckoned that for a technologically based career two science subjects are necessary (along with mathematics), in the fourth year, only 44 per cent of boys and 31 per cent of girls were taking two or more science subjects. By the fifth year, that had dropped to 40 per cent for boys and 24 per cent for girls. The differences between girls and boys were even more extreme in terms of the actual science subjects taken. For while girls preponderated in biology, there was only one girl for about every three boys doing physics at 'O' level, and one girl for every two boys doing 'O' level chemistry. Physics and chemistry thus remained 'boys' subjects'. Girls, said the regional conference briefing paper, 'by choosing not to take these subjects deny themselves career opportunities, and to a large extent shut themselves off from important aspects of the control of affairs'. In some cases, though, as a House of Commons Committee discovered to its horror,[24] girls were not even *offered* science subjects because of shortage of laboratory spaces. Shortage of physics teachers, too, has been a potent factor – though there are signs now that this is coming to an end. It seems also to be the case that many girls who start out by doing biology on its own find that they lack sufficient scientific background to understand what they are studying and end up by abandoning even biology.[25]

Partial remedies for this state of affairs might be to insist on everybody doing at least one science subject, or to offer a general science course combining physics, chemistry and biology, with optional 'modules' for specialists. But the reasons for the girls' failure to come forward in the sciences appear to be complex and deep-rooted, involving everything from notions of femininity to the prejudices of industry and lack of women teachers in these subjects. An interesting sidelight was thrown on this by work at Bradford University's School of Research in Education.[26] This showed that those girls who do take science at sixth-form level are, on average, outstandingly able and see themselves as less attractive than other girls.

In languages, however, girls seem to rule the roost. The number of 'O' and 'A' level passes in French has actually been dropping – at 'O' level from 95,000 in 1965 to 89,000 in 1974, and at 'A' level from 18,000 in 1965 to 17,000 in 1974 – and this during a period when passes have risen steeply in almost every other subject.[27] Even more striking, however, is the fact that while only 46 per cent of those doing French 'A' level in 1963 were boys, by 1974 this had shrunk to 34 per cent. The tendency for languages to become girls' territory is most marked in co-educational comprehensives – as also is the trend for girls to give a wide berth to physics and chemistry. The implication is that when both sexes are together girls try to be more feminine in an old-fashioned sense and boys to be more masculine.

In languages, as in maths, continuity is also a major problem. Because one school may pay little attention to what another does, children usually have to start again in secondary school even if they have done some French in primary school. If there is a middle school they may have to start from scratch three times. In these areas, not very surprisingly, there are fewer 'O' level passes than in parts of the country where students do a continuous five-year course.[28] Of eighty-three schools in the H.M.I. survey from which these facts are taken, only seven had consulted their feeder primary schools. Many boys are also giving up in the middle of French courses designed to take them to the age of sixteen, without achieving any of the objectives of the course.[29]

Apart from science, maths and languages, there are other great problems with the curriculum. The most basic is frequent failure to plan for a particular skill or subject right across the school, as *A Language for Life* suggested should be done for English. Things often move forward in an uncoordinated, jerky way. A humanities course, for example, may be introduced in year one, but very often without the consequent adjustment which should have been made to, say, history and geography courses in later years. Little account may be taken in planning a course of those who will drop it at fourteen. What use is it to a fourteen-year-old, inspectors are inclined to ask, to have studied British history from 55 B.C. to A.D. 1485?

Then again, there is the major question of the subjects that are left out and whether there is room to fit them in. As Matthew Arnold, poet and H.M.I., wrote in the nineteenth century:

> Fresh matters of instruction are continually being added to our school programmes; but it is well to remember that the recipient for this instruction, the child, remains as to age, capacity, and school time, what he was before, and that his age, capacity, and school time must in the end govern our proceedings. Undoubtedly, there is danger at present of his being over-urged and over-worked, of his being taught too many things, and not the best things for him.[30]

My own notebook of the regional conferences, are full of records of speakers who jumped to their feet to demand more time for the subjects in which they were themselves specialists. Successive speakers in Cardiff, for instance, advocated more concentration on Christianity, careers and Welsh – all of them subjects of great importance in the Principality. 'Man is very much a spiritual being, as well as having a mind and body', said the lady who wanted Christian education. Careers education and guidance should be introduced from the third form upwards, said the careers teacher. Only the Welsh language, said the Welsh language teacher, gave Welsh children an opportunity 'to identify with this piece of land that we are living on'. In a pluralist society some way must be found of accommodating special interests. Welsh is a good example. Yet where, one may wonder, will this ever end?

In terms of subjects with universal relevance, there seem to be three areas in which many people believe there should be more teaching and learning. One of these is the 'world of work', the subject of the next section. Another is careers education, coming up fast but often criticized in its present form. The third is made up of such 'adult' subjects as politics, sex education, or consumer affairs. All these are closely related, since all are directly involved with life after school.

Of the 'adult' subjects, consumer and 'administrative' education (teaching about such things as social security and mortgages) is beginning to improve. But the rest are honoured mainly by neglect. The National Child Development Study revealed that a quarter of sixteen-year-olds could not recall having received a basic education in the physiology of reproduction. Nearly half had no instruction on venereal disease. A Family Planning Association survey of sixth-formers in 1976 said that, although sex education was the most important way of preventing unwanted pregnancies, more than half had received no sex education at all. One third of the remainder said it was 'just touched on'.

Politics is ignored almost as effectively as sex. A Hansard Society survey of school leavers, completed in 1977, discovered that more than half could not name the foreign secretary. Forty-four per cent of those questioned thought the I.R.A. was a Protestant organization. A quarter thought the Conservatives favoured nationalization.

The reason for the schools' failure to tackle sex and politics – except sometimes by dull and mechanical descriptions – is probably because these subjects are so controversial. In politics, the charge of indoctrination is deeply feared by teachers. But one of the most interesting curricular events during the period of the Great Debate was the publication in *The Times Educational Supplement*[31] of a paper on political education written by two H.M.I.s. Arguing that the aim of political education should be the preservation and enhancement of democracy, they said that schools should give their pupils the knowledge and tools for responsible political participation. This might help to relieve society's cynicism about politics. To achieve this, mere 'civics' was not enough. Much more positive teaching should be attempted. And this, as the H.M.I.s were not slow to point out, involved some central questions about the nature of school life, 'Do we train young people to live in a democracy by talking to them excessively rather than inviting their views? Does repeated copying from textbooks or worksheets produce autonomous citizens?'

The ensuing correspondence and articles of commentary made fascinating reading. Some teachers felt that the inspectors were advocating genuine pupil power, others – more radical – that any move towards pupil power would be meaningless so long as adults remained in charge. But on the issue of indoctrination, the general view appeared to be that of the chairman of the Political Association: 'To be explicit, to have a planned course and a published syllabus, must surely be the best defence against the charge of indoctrination.' Political education, it seemed, might be on the way at last.

But one of the messages to be read from the present state of the curriculum is that if one subject grows another must diminish. This applies to politics as to anything else. The secondary curriculum is already overstuffed and, for many youngsters, seriously out of balance. The argument for a common framework is a strong one.

III: School and work

There is deep suspicion, amounting at times to antagonism, between the world of education and Britain's industrial employers. Discussions are carried on in an atmosphere of mutual fault-finding. John Methven, director general of the Confederation of British Industry, said in a speech made in the autumn of 1976:[32]

The question of standards dominates much thinking about education today, particularly at the schools level. Employers have contributed to this because there has, over recent years, been growing dissatisfaction among them at the standards of achievement in the basic skills reached by many school leavers, particularly those leaving at the official age ... Employers appreciate that advances in education have changed the character of the residual pool of ability in the schools and for this they have been prepared. [This was a reference to the growing number now going directly from school to higher and further education, with the consequence that those going from school to work may be of lesser ability than previously. However, the fact remains that, after one of the longest periods of compulsory education in Europe, many young people seem ill equipped for almost any kind of employment and woefully ignorant about the basic economic facts.

The teachers, for their part, were issuing statements like this:

How many employers have been inside a school in the last ten years, let alone spent a week there appraising what goes on? How many rely on folklore and their own partial memories?[33]

This mutual antipathy has roots going back two hundred years. It originated in a rift between the liberal arts and manufacturing industry which was peculiar to this country and owed a good deal of its width and depth to our unusually rigid class-structure.

In the eighteenth century, Oxford and Cambridge were deeply slothful institutions, the Oxford colleges in particular being overwhelmingly concerned with providing a secure living for their Fellows.[34]. The scientific revolution passed them by and, except in mathematics, they were thoroughly backward-looking. Here, for example, is Cambridge's Professor of Chemistry, giving evidence to a Royal Commission in 1850–52.

Hitherto the study of Chemistry has not only been neglected but discouraged in the University, as diverting the attention of pupils from what have been considered their proper academical studies.

When science finally reached Oxford and Cambridge, it did so in a big way. There can be little doubt that in pure, as opposed to applied, science these two universities are today pre-eminent and that the universities generally are the pacemakers in scientific inquiry. Technology, however, fared very differently. After the Great Exhibition of 1851, and even more after the

Paris Exhibition of 1867, there was growing alarm at the way in which Britain had lost its lead in design and manufacture. Practical scientific education now became the cry, not because of the position of science in contemporary thought but because it was needed for efficient manufacture.

'One unhappy consequence of this narrowly pragmatic attitude to science,' wrote Sir Eric Ashby, 'was that scientific education tended to be regarded as more suitable for artisans and the lower middle classes than for the governing classes.' The University of London and colleges in such cities as Manchester, Birmingham and Leeds grew up to serve the needs of industry and the lower middle classes. Mechanics institutes evolved to provide a technical education for the working classes.

This division between Oxford and Cambridge and the rest, would not perhaps have mattered very much had it not been for the great dominance of Oxford and Cambridge in the latter part of the nineteenth century, particularly as asserted through examinations. From Oxford's earliest experiments with school examinations in 1857, there had been a strong tendency to discount practical subjects in favour of the classics and the humanities generally.[35] This remained the trend in the public schools, who now saw their main task as the provision of educated gentlemen for the administration of the empire. As far as these were concerned, technology was something that other people took care of.

Technological education continued to grow in its less glamorous way, both in the institutes and newer universities, finally reaching Oxford and Cambridge and getting a fresh boost when such universities as Bradford and Salford were formed in the 1960s from the former colleges of advanced technology. But technology has never acquired its own prestigious institutions as in France, Germany or the United States. The position remains much as Sir Eric Ashby described it in 1958:

Technology is of the earth, earthy; it is susceptible to pressure from industry and government departments; it is under an obligation to deliver the goods. And so the crude engineer, the mere technologist (the very adjectives are symptoms of the attitude) are tolerated in universities because the State and industry are willing to finance them. Tolerated, but not assimilated; for the traditional don is not yet willing to admit that technologists have anything intrinsic to contribute to academic life.

Even the formation of a network of thirty polytechnics from 1965 onwards has done little if anything to redress this balance, for though the polytechnics were intended to provide a more practical type of education than the universities they have so far failed to win anything approaching university prestige. Some of the polytechnics have themselves tended to emulate the universities in a process of 'academic drift' which is carrying them away from the applied sciences and towards 'pure' research and teaching.[36]

At this stage in its singular history, therefore, technology stands low both in class terms and in terms of our intellectual hierarchies.

It was against this background that Sir Alex Smith, early in 1976, delivered a lecture[37] containing many thoughts which later became central to the Great Debate. Before becoming director of Manchester Polytechnic (and chairman of the Schools Council), Sir Alex had been director of research for Rolls-Royce. This had given him an unusual opportunity to scrutinize the grass on both sides of the fence and he now spoke with some authority. First he listed symptoms of economic decline. Illustrating each in depressing detail, he noted the steady, underlying growth in unemployment; growth in imports of machinery (a highly significant indicator of failure in technology); a decline in Britain's share of manufactured goods; a decline in our export-to-import ratio and – though this is in reverse as I write – the falling value of our currency. He then compared these to graphic instances of our failure to provide adequate education in technology.

There had been a fall, said Sir Alex, in the number taking higher certificates and diplomas in technology. At the same time, the number studying for degrees in the United Kingdom had grown considerably – from 200,000 in 1965 to 275,000 in 1973. But among the greater number now taking advanced courses of all kinds (here he gave figures or England and Wales only), the total studying engineering and technology had actually declined. The number following social, administrative and business studies, on the other hand, had almost doubled. Breaking these figures down again, Sir Alex arrived at the following conclusion: for every new student enrolling in 1973 to study the vitally important subject of production engineering there were five new students in economics, twelve in law, sixteen in sociology and *forty* in business or commerce. (To this may be added the fact, among many others pointing in the same direction, that out of every hundred new graduates in 1975 only thirteen went straight into industry.[38])

Developments in day release were equally striking. In 1964 the Henniker-Heaton report[39] had recommended that the number of boys and girls obtaining day release from work for further education should be doubled from 250,000 to 500,000, at the rate of 50,000 a year. 'It is vitally important for the future well-being of the nation and for our industrial prosperity that the proportion receiving day release should be rapidly increased,' said the report. '... we appeal for the interest and active assistance of every individual who is in a position to further this work in his personal, official or industrial capacity. The task is of immediate national importance.'

What had happened since that appeal, Sir Alex said, was a steady decline in the number of under-eighteens obtaining day release. Only 20 per cent of Britain's young workers now got release compared to 85 per cent in West Germany. (Figures published by the Engineering Industry Training Board in 1977 showed that this British decline in day release, at any rate in engineering, was still continuing apace.[40])

Sir Alex was careful not to suggest that there was any causal link between our industrial misfortunes and the current pattern of enrolment in higher education. The effect of that pattern would show itself in the future 'and the omens are obviously not good':

But both trends, I think, can be attributed to the same underlying social cause – to the lack of esteem given to skills in doing, making, designing, developing, manufacturing, compared with the high esteem given to academic study and scholarship, to analysis and to research as the proper pursuits for the ablest minds.

This, then, was the state of affairs when Mr Callaghan made his speech later in 1976. But what precisely was to be done?

The simple, commonsense approach would appear to have been to encourage schools to teach in a way that would enhance the prestige of industry and technology and so, one might hope, encourage economic growth in years to come. Some, as we shall see in a moment, did advocate this approach. But the response to it from teachers and many liberal-minded people was one of extreme hostility – to the confusion, I suspect, of those citizens who were not directly involved in the argument. All becomes relatively clear, however, when one, central fact is apprehended. It is a fact which was never, to my knowledge, spelled out clearly during the Great Debate, nor perhaps realized by many of the participants, and it is simply this: despite general agreement that national bankruptcy would be a bad thing, all the solutions suggested were by definition political. What we were hearing, though in a confused and muffled way, was the clash of political ideologies.

Lest anyone should doubt this point – which is basic to the rest of this chapter – let me outline two rival prospectuses for our industrial future. I have in front of me a document[41] prepared for candidates in forthcoming European elections by thirty-nine European environmental bodies, several of them British. It calls for a 'mature pattern' of economic growth, based on the concepts of thrift and sustainability and on individual craftsmanship rather than 'throwaway production'. The contrasting view is that growth should be accelerated, with consumption of fossil fuel at whatever pace is demanded by industry (consider Britain's North Sea oil policy) and possibly with the addition of energy from fast-breeder nuclear reactors. Now, if the first prospectus is political – which it is, openly and avowedly, and no matter how idealistic it may seem – then so, in logic, is the second. We are not so apt to realize that this is political because the maximum-growth view is widely accepted and therefore seems a part of daily life rather than politics. Similarly in education, the view that schools have a duty to endorse the aims of industry appears at first to be non-political. It is in fact political to the highest degree, and for the same reason: it involves the endorsement of one particular economic prospectus.

This is extremely important, partly because the Callaghan view of industry is repudiated by those of more radical persuasion (as we shall see in a moment) and partly because, if one political intrusion in the curriculum is allowed, then another might later be substituted for it. A right-wing government might wish to tell the children that the economy could only flourish if the trades unions were extirpated. A left-wing government could teach that only the bosses, red in tooth and claw, stood between the nation and prosperity.

But what precisely did the government intend? Nobody made it plainer than Mr Callaghan himself. He wished the schools to create a favourable impression of industry, just as the C.B.I. and the maximum-growth lobby advocated. He spelled it out like this to an N.U.T. careers convention in October 1977:

It can only be through the wealth that industry creates that we can hope to maintain and improve our standard of living ... It shows how far we have lost our way that, in the country where the industrial revolution began, the achievements of industry and those who work there are so often disparaged ... All in positions of influence whether in education, the media, trades unions, professional bodies or the government, have a responsibility to bring about a change in our national attitudes.

On the intimately related question of manpower supply – or, to put it unkindly, 'factory fodder' – there were also indications that the political platforms of government and C.B.I. had much in common. Here, for example, are the opening paragraphs in a press release issued by the Department of Education and Science on 8 September 1977:

Industry, the wealth-creating sector, needs happy, healthy, skilled workers, Mr Gordon Oakes, Minister of State for Education and Science, told the Standing Conference of Regional Advisory Councils for Further Education, in Scarborough today.

The aim was to equip industry to face a competitive world in which British industry was failing to keep pace. Since 1962 the U.K. share of major industrialized countries' exports had fallen from 15·3 per cent to 9·3 per cent.

'The positive approach is to create a climate for reversing this trend. Those of us in education have a big part to play.'

The anger aroused by this approach makes little sense until it is acknowledged that even within the mainstream of British politics there is an alternative view. This, briefly, is that industry *as it now exists* has no entitlement to automatic respect. Len Murray, general secretary of the Trades Union Congress, made the point with some force at the same N.U.T. conference that Mr Callaghan addressed.[42] First he expressed regret that 'many of the jobs society wants individuals to do offer little in themselves beyond the wage packet'. Then he went on:

It is no use preaching sermons to young people – or to adults, for that matter – about the dignity or the value of labour, if all they have to do is guide a piece of metal into a press and tread on a foot pedal 1000 times a day … Most systems of work tend to reduce individual initiative and to favour authoritarian forms of supervision. Many workplaces and work systems are unpleasant; most present hazards to health and safety, and some industries still have appalling records in these respects … It is not the job of education to ensure that young people settle for the *status quo*.

This is a political view. It is shared by many teachers and above all by the leadership of the N.U.T. They believe that the government is not only intruding in the curriculum, which is unacceptable, but that it is intruding for the sake of views which are equally unacceptable. In this context, it is worth noting that almost all the teachers' spokesmen have come to achieve that position through trades union activity. Meanwhile, the teacher unions, in contrast to many industrial unions, are in continual hot pursuit of professional status. In this connection they share the general distaste for industry felt by intellectuals and professional people. Thus their professional position, through an interesting and possibly unique mechanism, reinforces deeply felt trades union doubts about the employers' version of industry.

Another consideration has also prompted the teachers in their hostility to the industrialists. This is unemployment among the young.

Unemployment among sixteen- and seventeen-year-olds rose by 120 per cent between January 1972 and January 1975, compared with a rise of 45 per cent among the working population as a whole. This age-group constituted 5·4 per cent of those unemployed in January 1971 and 9 per cent in January 1977. Girls and immigrant groups were most affected.[43] There is no realistic projection which shows unemployment among those under twenty years old dropping to less than 100,000 within the foreseeable future.

This has important consequences *inside* schools in almost all parts of the country. According to the N.U.T.'s preparatory pamphlet for the regional conferences,[44] 'prospects of unemployment or jobs they find unattractive have an inevitable influence on the attitudes of young people ... A major contributory cause of young people's ill-preparedness for work and low motivation in school is their awareness, in many cases, of the lack of any meaningful and fulfilling employment for many of them.' Yet here was industry, both telling the schools to produce willing workers and simultaneously accusing them, by implication – as did John Methven in his remarks on unemployable school leavers – of creating youth unemployment. On the contrary, the evidence seemed to show[45] that employers were reluctant to go to the expense of taking on trainees when it was possible to 'poach' skilled labour elsewhere. Britain's record for allowing unemployment to fall on the young was the worst of any country in Europe.[46] Surely industry should take some responsibility for this instead of seeking to blame the schools?[47] And surely the root cause of unemployment lay anyway in lack of jobs?

The teachers were also worried on more obviously educational grounds about the claims of industry. The anxiety here went back to the potential conflict between society and the individual, dismissed with such easy confidence by Mr Callaghan. The teachers felt it was their duty to attend to the needs of the individual. As Dr John Rae, headmaster of Westminster School, put it, in his fortnightly column in *The Times Educational Supplement* on 3 December 1976:

> We were brought up to believe that education should, in the words of the Universal Declaration of Human Rights, be 'directed to the full development of human personality'. And we suspect that this aim cannot be reconciled with the sort of measures that government may think necessary to achieve economic viability.

By September the following year Dr Rae was writing: '. . . the conflict that is now developing between national requirements and teachers' attitudes is real.'

But even if Dr Rae was right, as was undoubtedly the case, there seemed no justification for mutual ignorance. Teachers were worried that industry knew little about the schools. The government was even more worried that the teachers were innocent about industry. A cure for this condition (see final chapter) became one of the key aims of policy. That the attempt could be worthwhile was shown by a simple experiment in Coventry.[48] Complaints from the local engineering employers association indicated that while the intelligence-test scores of new apprentices had remained constant over the past five years, standards in literacy and numeracy had fallen steadily. In response to this, and with the blessing of the local authority, two teachers embarked on a series of regular visits to engineering firms to see what was really required of their pupils. The results were remarkably interesting, for while they showed that the schools were indeed failing the engineering firms in many ways, so also were the engineering firms failing the individual. The engineers complained that the schools were teaching 'metric' maths, even though industry seemed likely to stick with imperial measures till the end of the century; calculators, much used at school, were frowned upon by training officers; various useful methods of calculation had not been taught, or not taught well enough. Industry, on the other hand, could not attract the candidates it wanted because of poor conditions. Pay in offices and banks was now as good as in engineering and life a great deal more comfortable. 'The abler young were naturally going where the pay, perks and working environment were best,' said *The Times Educational Supplement*. Each side was letting down the other.

This eyeball-to-eyeball approach, in which young people might as readily be involved as adults, seemed to hold out the possibility that the omnipresent politics of the matter could at least be addressed in a spirit of greater realism. To ease the transition from school to adult life and to help them match their own ambitions with reality, what the young needed above all appeared to be direct, personal and meaningful contact with the confusing 'world of work'. Fifty years earlier the philosopher A. N. Whitehead had written:[49]

A factory, with its machinery, its community of operatives, its social service to the general population, its dependence upon organizing and designing genius, its potentialities as a source of wealth to the holders of its stock is an organism exhibiting a variety of vivid values. What we want to train is the habit of apprehending such an organism in its completeness.

People will always argue over the value of values, but to apprehend something of industry in its completeness would seem a reasonably uncontroversial aim for education. This relatively value-free approach is very different from the proselytizing one that Mr Callaghan openly advocated. But it must also be remembered that when one element is introduced into the curriculum another must be dropped. Only a limited amount can be achieved by 'refocusing the content and approach' within existing subjects.[50] It is also essential that in future discussions there should be clarity of mind about the difference between education and the direction of labour.

So much in conclusion: this section cannot end, however, without a brief remark on vocational education.

For many years, vocational study has been regarded as mere training and quite distinct from education. Why training and education should be so utterly distinct remains mysterious. The confusion has been increased because the word 'vocational' is often taken to mean the same as 'practical'. Both have been held in low esteem. Part of the theory behind comprehensive reform was to extend the opportunities for practical study so as to favour technological advance. The resulting technological advance appears to have been small (why, otherwise, a Great Debate?); and the status of practical subjects remains low. Unbelievably, and by a recent resolution, the Royal Institution of Chartered Surveyors will not accept 'O' level technical drawing as an entry qualification. The Royal Institute of British Architects will not accept more than one 'practical' 'O' level among the five subjects it demands at 'O' and 'A' level. The Institute of Housing accepts no practical subjects, not even woodwork. And so on and so forth through a vast range of professional institutes. Nevertheless, some progress was made during the Great Debate. A consensus seemed to emerge that training too early for a particular line of work might turn out, in a time of rapid change, to limit an adult's life-chances. And many efforts were made to remove the stigma from the purely practical.

Other developments outside school appeared to be pushing in the same direction. One element in the government's response to youth unemployment was the creation, under the umbrella of the Manpower Services Commission, of a body named the Training Services Agency. This began simply by trying to create new opportunities for young people; but it very quickly came to interest itself in the actual curriculum of the training offered to those who had left school. It seemed certain that the work of the T.S.A. would in time tend to push schoolteachers in a more practical direction.

IV: Standards and how to judge them

Controversy over standards has arisen partly because of genuine doubt, partly because the matter is political. Reformists, generally Labour-inclined, are under some obligation to think standards are improving; counter-reformists, more often than not Conservative, believe the opposite. Fact and opinion are hopelessly entwined. This situation persists because the information available is more a set of clues than hard-and-fast evidence. The question therefore arises as to whether we should not try to measure standards in some more convincing way than happens now. This, if it were possible, might simultaneously settle the argument over standards, show where more effort should be made, and provide a means by which the education service could be accountable, in a way that it is not at present because of lack of information. In this section, I shall review the evidence on standards, some of which has been touched on already; consider public examinations and possibilities for reform; and look at some other important changes already in the pipeline. Since much of the subject is technical I shall try to be brief, rather than pursuing each twist and turn of the statistical hare. I hope that footnotes and other references to sources will allow those with a serious interest to take the topic further.

On standards, there are four main questions, all posed by the Black Paper writers. What are the effects of informal methods in primary schools; of mixed-ability teaching in secondary schools; and of comprehensive reorganization? Are standards in general rising or falling?[51]

I have already attempted an answer to the first two questions in the section on the curriculum. It seems in summary that there is not much to choose between one teaching method and another. Home background and the skill and experience of teachers are more important. Where informal primary methods and mixed-ability teaching fall down is usually where they are wrongly applied – directionless teaching in primary schools, for example, or a tendency in mixed-ability teaching to treat widely differing individuals as a single group. It is also worth noting a point once made to me by Professor Paul Hirst of Cambridge University's Institute of Education – that the new and less formal methods of education were devised precisely because the more abstract teaching methods long used with able children were seen to be failing when applied to the whole ability range. Modern methods are an attempt to cope with failure, rather than its cause. It follows from this that for the sake of some children at least it will be worth persevering in the effort to help teachers to understand these methods and apply them better than is often done at present.

The question of the effect of comprehensive reorganization on standards remains wide open. The only serious attempts to make a judgement have been based on comparisons between the exam results of unreorganized and reorganized schools – though this, as I shall argue in a moment, is probably not the best way to make a worthwhile assessment. Professor Robin Pedley of Southampton University, a comprehensive lobbyist, published the results of an early survey, favourable to comprehensives, in 1969.[52] These were savagely attacked in the Black Papers. General opinion today is that Pedley's schools were not sufficiently representative of the population for firm conclusions to be drawn. In 1972, a study of twelve individual comprehensives[53] (which were not intended to be representative) found that more fifth-year pupils were staying on and gaining exam passes than expected from national statistics (a big plus mark in terms of the objectives of the comprehensive sector). At sixth-form level, performance was roughly in line with the national average, given the 'characteristics' of those staying on.

Since then, most of the discussion has come from Mr Raymond Baldwin, chairman of governors at Manchester Grammar School and a Black Paper contributor. In a computation of exam results published in 1975,[54] he sought to show that comprehensives achieved substantially fewer exam passes at the higher levels than grammar and secondary moderns combined. As so often happens, conservatives took these figures as gospel while liberal statisticians opened up serious holes in them. Drawing the criticisms together and adding new findings of his own, Nigel Wright has had no difficulty in showing that Baldwin's figures did not allow for creaming, for methods of reorganization that involved 'comprehensivization' of *all* secondary moderns but of only *some* grammar schools, or for the differing social composition of reorganized and unreorganized areas

(areas which had gone comprehensive were more likely to be either rural or working class). The net effect was to invalidate Baldwin's argument, though without, of course, settling the issue.

Baldwin published further figures in the 1977 Black Paper. In these, he tried to make allowance for creaming, by moving 7000 grammar school pupils (and their results) out of the unreorganized and into the comprehensive sector. This still left 14·51 per cent of those in unreorganized schools getting one or more 'A' level, compared with just 11·59 per cent in the comprehensives. The figures for those with at least two 'A' levels were: unreorganized, 11·68 per cent, comprehensive 8·76 per cent, and for those with at least three 'A' levels, 7·9 per cent in the unreorganized schools and 5·36 per cent in the comprehensives. Baldwin's 7000, however, represented just 3 per cent of the grammar school population, and only 2 per cent of grammar school calibre pupils in the comprehensives. As Dr Desmond Nuttall, secretary of the (C.S.E.) Middlesex Regional Examining Board, pointed out, 'It seems difficult to believe that, nationwide, comprehensive schools lose only 2 per cent of the full ability range.'[55] Once again Baldwin had made no allowance for class differences between reorganized and unreorganized sectors. Nor, said Dr Nuttall, had he reckoned with the fact that one third of 'A' level entries were in colleges of further education. It was likely that a higher proportion of these came from the comprehensive than the unreorganized sector. This meant that Baldwin was not comparing like with like, and that his methods 'though steadily improving, still leave much to be desired'. The gap, if it were not closed by the factors ignored, would certainly be much narrowed.

Interestingly enough, the issue of *The Times Educational Supplement* that carried Nuttall's article reported an apparently punctilious analysis from a midlands county which showed a reverse image of Baldwin's findings – 15 per cent of the comprehensive pupils getting one or more 'A' levels, only 11 per cent in the unreorganized schools.[56] But this was a county where, contrary to the usual pattern, it was the predominantly working-class areas which had retained the grammar schools. This raises the possibility that social class is more important in deciding exam results than either segregation or its absence. There is so far nothing to prove that academic standards in comprehensives are either higher or lower than in the schools of the unreorganized sector. Those who support comprehensives must argue on other grounds than exam results. But, equally, there is no case for vilifying the comprehensives because of their exam results.

Most passion of all, perhaps, goes into the question of whether or not standards are falling, and here the evidence is partly reassuring, partly inconclusive. The main difficulty is that it seems impossible to make valid comparisons between the present day and the period before the Second World War. It is to this period that many memories now return, as if to a golden age, ignoring the fact that complaints about falling standards were almost as plentiful then as they are now. But it is possible to make some general statements about the past thirty years.

In reading, as we have seen, the Bullock report found that standards had improved since 1948 (from a low war-time base). But results of N.F.E.R. tests in 1970 and 1971 (see above p. 89) implied at least a stutter in that improvement. New results from the National Foundation for Educational Research[57] reveal unequivocally that up to 1975 those standards were once more on the move upward.

This is the strongest evidence yet, so far as the primary schools are concerned, that the Great Debate was called after the process of self-correction had begun. These figures will be discussed in detail in the H.M.I. survey of primary schools, due for publication late in 1978. But one interesting point which can be noted now is that the margins of error in N.F.E.R. tests in 1964 and 1975 were very small, while in 1971 they were very large. This means that a straight line drawn on a graph between the 1964 and 1975 results passes through the area of uncertainty for 1971. In other words, it is possible – though hunch tells one the opposite – that reading standards have improved continuously at a steady rate and that the 1971 stutter was non-

existent. It has to be emphasized, however, that only silent reading skills of a mechanical kind have been tested up to now.
There is, of course, a good deal more than this to reading.

On writing there is no reliable evidence.

On mathematics, surprisingly in view of its definiteness as a
subject, there is also considerable lack of evidence. But a test
for the B.B.C.'s Man Alive programme in 1977 – conducted with
the help of the N.F.E.R. – showed that the performance of
fourteen-year-olds appeared to have worsened substantially
since 1964. (There was a similar fall-off in some other European
countries, with a rather greater decline in West Germany; the
U.S.A. stayed the same; Japan showed massive improvement. In
science, Britain had improved since 1970.) This is just one piece
of evidence, suggestive rather than conclusive, but there is not
much doubt that the overall situation in maths is poor to mid-
dling. Modern maths, however, has not apparently added to the
difficulties – even though it sometimes puts pleasure (or at any
rate avoidance of fear) far higher on its list of priorities than
'old' maths and may be more concerned with giving its pupils a
sense of the utility of numbers than with solving particular
problems. The H.M.I.'s preparatory paper[58] for the Great
Debate said that in the few instances where evidence was available 'there appears to be very little to choose between the attainments of those who have followed traditional and modern
courses, even where the designers might not have placed increased numerical competence very high on their list of aims.

Foreign languages are beyond all doubt the great disaster
area of modern state education, though whether standards are
dropping or merely abysmal is open to question. The main
reason for failure here is that a subject previously taught to
only the most-able has been extended rapidly to children of all
ability. In preparing a recent report[59] H.M.I.s visited eighty-
three representative schools, as noted above (p. 125). In 'all but
a few' of the schools, they found, among other defects, underperformance at all levels of ability in reading, writing, speaking
and understanding the spoken word (all the four skills involved
in learning a foreign language); the setting of 'impossible or

pointless tasks for average (and in particular less-able) pupils; and 'their abandonment of modern language learning at the first opportunity'. Some less-able pupils simply covered the same ground year after year. Sometimes there were no schemes of work at all. In one inner-city school 'little was being done to challenge able pupils; no attempt was being made to cater for the wide range of ability . . . language lessons were noisy and sometimes quite out of control; very few pupils continued beyond the option stage, and even these were relatively unsuccessful in public examinations'.

There was, however, one significant improvement. In Inner London, where teacher turnover was more extreme in the early 1970s than elsewhere in the country, the verbal reasoning score of eleven-year-olds dropped sharply, causing a good deal of worry. But by 1975, as school staffs became more stable, scores on the same tests crept back up to the national average. This was another piece of evidence that the Great Debate had set the pendulum swinging rather late in the day.

On the major question of what the results of public examinations tell us about national standards, there are two opinions. The former is held by the N.U.T. and Labour governments generally. It is basically that the enormous increase in the number of certificates awarded for G.C.E. and C.S.E. mean that teachers and their students are doing better. One of the figures most often quoted with approval is that eight out of ten school leavers are today achieving some kind of public qualification compared with five out of ten a decade ago. Not only this, the proportion leaving school with 'A' levels has crept up to the 15 per cent mark, and those taking five or more 'O' levels at the higher grades are nearing 10 per cent of the total. There have been heavy increases in the number getting higher grades of C.S.E. or middle grades of 'O' level – from 14 per cent in 1964–5 to 25 per cent in 1974–5. Average grades have also improved substantially.[60] All this is regarded as a great leap forward in productivity.

The Doubting Thomas view is generally held by educational conservatives. They point out that almost half of exam candidates offer only one or two 'O' level or C.S.E. papers which is not really very much. The lower grades of C.S.E. are virtually meaningless, at any rate to employers. The increase in the number achieving one or two passes may be brought about by the fact that all now have to stay on at school till sixteen (the age at which 'O' level and C.S.E. are taken) and not because pupils actually know more. More middle-grade passes are being achieved, they believe, simply because comprehensives are keener to enter marginal candidates than were the unreorganized sector. There is also suspicion that exams are easier to pass. The most striking piece of evidence here comes from a Schools Council study[61] by Dr Alan Willmott, of the N.F.E.R., which did indeed show a slip of one third of a grade in G.C.E. standards between 1968 and 1973. There was also a slip, though a smaller one, in C.S.E. But this finding was much disputed. It was arrived at by matching pupils' success in G.C.E. and C.S.E. against a standard reference test, thus showing that pupils of the same ability were doing better in exams in 1973. Some G.C.E. boards said that the reference test itself was hopelessly inaccurate. Some teachers felt that if pupils of a given ability were doing better, this might be because the schools were doing a better job. The whole area remains murky and there is likely to be fresh controversy when results for 1974 are published (perhaps in advance of the present volume). These will show a slippage of up to one eighth of a grade within a single year, raising once more the possibility that examiners are rewarding the same work with higher grades.

There is, I think, some merit in both the liberal and the conservative view of what exam results can tell us. The conservative view, however, can hardly account for the greater number passing at 'A' level. Here, at least, more people must know more, if only for the day of the exam. In general, however, the problems of interpreting results arise because public examinations, which are intended to measure the success of individuals, are being used as a measure of the whole school-system. They are simply not suitable for this. One reason is their great variety. They tell us that more young people are getting a bigger dose of school, which we knew already, but tell us little about the quality of learning. Another drawback is that one fifth of the school population is treated by the exam system as not worth testing. This means, as a House of Commons committee found,[62] that the standards achieved by lower-ability children are at present quite unknowable.

Before considering what alternatives there are, I should like to pause for a moment to look at the effect of exams on individuals, for this is where much of the controversy over exams in fact lies, and it is from this, as well as from a desire to control and measure the educational system, that proposals for reform arise.

One of the main arguments for traditional exams is that they act as an incentive to learning, obliging a student to get properly on top of his subject, even the parts of it he doesn't like. That this actually happens, at least among the most successful, was confirmed by a survey I carried out for *The Sunday Times*[63] of the country's leading 200 industrialists and of 100 prize-winning novelists and poets. Over 80 per cent of the industrialists (though fewer of the writers) believed the work they had done for exams had been not only helpful to them in their careers but of permanent value to them in their personal lives. Among other advantages claimed for exams is that they give a student a realistic way of rating his own performance. Teachers like exams for many of the same reasons. They provide a shared motive for work and, in external exams, a common enemy in the shape of the examiner. As far as employers are concerned, exams act as a preliminary sorting mechanism, so that it is not necessary for the school leaver to traipse from employer to employer, taking battery after battery of aptitude and attainment tests.[64] They also help sort out those who will go on to higher education.

Those who dislike exams, at least in their present form, try to stand most of these arguments on their head. First, they say – and quite correctly – that an exam which may determine a child's future in a single afternoon is a great ordeal. Is it a necessary one? There is also, they say, an inbuilt competitive element in traditional exams. This is because they function by sorting candidates into a ranking order, instead of simply certifying that they possess some particular skill or knowledge (as a driving test does, for instance). The conflict here is another of the great touchstones of attitude to education. For a competitive, 'norm-referenced' exam – as the jargon has it – may be seen as the climax of a traditional education. A non-competitive, 'criterion-referenced' exam is compatible with progressive ideals. But these are chased out of secondary education, certainly out of its upper reaches, by the all-pervasive system of norm-referenced G.C.E. and C.S.E. As for employers, the critics say that they are irresponsible in their use of exam results. Where there is a surplus of labour they push their requirements up and up so that we get a crazy qualifications spiral as at present, with potential hairdressers being asked for their 'O' levels. And in the last resort, it is qualities of character that employers want, even if they use exams as an initial barrier.[65]

It has also been shown that 'A' level grades, though used as a basis for selecting students for university and polytechnic, bear remarkably little relationship to the degree finally obtained.[66] This is particularly pronounced in the arts subjects where competition for places is fiercest. 'A' level requirements are pushed up and up despite their uselessness as predictors. No other form of prediction, however, seems any more successful.

Exams can be unfair to the individual in many ways. As we have seen, the grades awarded for the same work quite possibly differ from year to year as a result of marking drift. There may also be a tendency among some boards, in mass-entry subjects at 'A' level, to award a particular grade to a particular percentage of the entry rather than because of the standard reached[67] by the individual candidate. This does not seem to happen at 'O' level or in C.S.E. Marking of individual papers is also somewhat random. In G.C.E. and C.S.E. it is accurate only to one grade on either side of that actually achieved so that 'a candidate awarded a grade 3 might well have received a grade 2 or a grade 4 under different, but equally valid, conditions'.[68]

This could make all the difference between success and failure in entering a career. Some subjects are also much harder than others. Research by the (G.C.E.) Joint Matriculation Board[69] in Manchester has shown that English language and literature, art, biology and geography are all comparatively easy to do well in. History, mathematics, French, chemistry and physics are difficult. In C.S.E. Mode III there is also a serious possibility that despite attempts at external moderation some schools get away with far more lenient marking than others.

As for the learning engaged in for exams, that, say the critics, is mostly dull memorization, with a premium put on the power of reproducing other people's ideas and positive penalties for evidence of creative talent or personal discovery. Teachers teach to the exam and nothing else. The result, allegedly, is a blotting-paper student, programmed for competition.

Radicals conclude from this that exams should be abolished, perhaps to be replaced by tests in maths and English. Conservatives remain unmoved. Liberals want reform.

Of the reformists, few have any very impressive remedies for the unfairness and inaccuracy of assessment by exam. But there is a growing desire among teachers to supplement exam results with a profile of each pupil, giving a fuller account of his attainments, interests and aspirations. Whenever such schemes have been discussed,[70] or specimen profiles published,[71] teacher interest has been keen. The profile system would mean that school-leavers of lower ability would have something to show for their years of school. It could even be used, if it worked, as a substitute for exams. The case against profiles is that they might well lack credibility, since entries would depend on the opinions of individual teachers.

One of the leading motives of those working for reform of public exams has been to improve the quality of learning while retaining the advantages of incentive. A main tool in C.S.E., for instance, is continuous assessment rather than the one-off exam. Under continuous assessment, it is day-to-day progress which is being judged and so by implication valued. Another of the most important ideas behind C.S.E. is that teachers should be free to choose the work most useful for their pupils – as they are under Modes II and III – and to assess them in that, rather than by their performances in a syllabus chosen by people perhaps remote from them and marching to a totally alien drum-beat.

This brings us back once again to the central question of control. For perhaps *the* most important function of the traditional external exam, though it is seldom acknowledged, is to control the curriculum. The three levels at which reform has recently been proposed are, as we have seen: sixteen-plus (to heal the breach between G.C.E. and C.S.E. by combining them into a single system); at seventeen-plus (the proposal here is for the C.E.E. exam, advocated as a target for the non-academic sixth-former who may at present spend his one year in the sixth form trying to convert C.S.E.s into 'O' levels); and at 'A' level (the attempt to broaden the syllabus from three to five subjects through 'N' and 'F' exams). At each level these proposals represented in their original forms an attempt to gain control for the schools by removing it from external G.C.E. examiners. That meant in effect the universities, for though many of those who sit on the all-important G.C.E. subject panels are teachers, there is evidence to show that teachers at sixth-form level identify heavily with university goals.[72] What are under threat, as far as they and the universities are concerned, are traditional, academic values. These are very often associated with the three-hour essay paper still favoured at 'A' level and in degree exams.

The question of control of public exams, even though it arises largely from the teachers' desire to do their best by individuals, relates of course to the question of how to assess the whole school system. Again, the key issue is one of control. G.C.E. is designed to control the curriculum; C.S.E. is designed to free the curriculum, releasing the student from the 'backwash' effect of exams. Neither measures the system adequately. Proposals for doing so fall neatly into 'controlling' or 'non-controlling' categories.

Throughout the period of the Great Debate the Conservative party advocated national examinations, most probably at the ages of seven, eleven and fourteen. One of the purposes of the exam would inescapably be its backwash, that is to say, the definition and enforcement of a common core, probably ranging from basic literacy and numeracy at the earlier ages to some minimum range of skills required by the school leaver. (Most Conservative spokesmen would also like to see these results published school by school, so as to act as a stimulus and sanction to the unsuccessful.)

The main argument against a national exam is that teachers would accommodate themselves to the straitjacket, letting the minimum of the tests become a maximum. Precisely this, occurred late in the nineteenth century when there was a system of paying the teachers by their pupils' results in standard tests. This prompted Matthew Arnold to write: 'Admitting the stimulus of the test examination to be salutary, we may therefore yet say that when it is overemployed it has two faults: it tends to make the instruction mechanical, and to set a bar to duly extending it.'

In the U.S.A., where minimum tests are now being introduced in a majority of states as part of a 'back-to-basics' movement, the same tendency has been observed.[73] In the hope of raising standards in Britain, the Conservatives, it is now said by educational liberals, are prepared to run the risk of narrowing and impoverishing school life. The further argument against publishing the results for individual schools is that these would be fairly meaningless, and certainly wide open to misinterpretation, if they did not allow for such factors as creaming or the social composition of a catchment area.

While this argument has raged, many local authorities have begun to introduce their own tests. Examples come from areas as diverse as Lancashire, Coventry, Croydon and Redbridge. In many cases, the aim is not to impose a curriculum but to see how well the schools are doing in achieving their own objectives. This, though it may in the end lead towards some more general and rational approach to the curriculum, is on the whole acceptable to teachers; and it has the great benefit of letting the local authorities know which schools or subjects need extra help. Unless these tests become uniform, however, they do not take us much nearer to any estimate of national standards. There is also the possibility that what we are seeing today is merely the first stage of incipient test-mania, through which preparation for tests and practice in tests could come to dominate school work as much as through any national exam. (The Inner London Education Authority has an interesting variant in which schools are invited to assess their own work by answering a series of difficult and thought-provoking questions.[74] In schools where I have seen this in operation, the process of self-appraisal has had the excellent effect of alerting teachers to unsuspected weaknesses.)

Local-authority attempts to measure standards are, so far, patchy and may become problematical if they begin to pre-empt control over the curriculum in any devious or accidental way. (This is not to imply at this stage of the discussion that nobody should control the curriculum, merely that there will be chaos if it is not controlled, whether by teachers, local authorities or even central government, in an above-board manner, open to discussion.)

There is one serious attempt already underway to monitor national standards in a manner specifically intended not to impinge on the curriculum. This is the work of the Assessment of Performance Unit.

The A.P.U. was set up in 1974 under the wing of Her Majesty's Inspectorate, and spent its first four years deciding what to test and how to test it. Its aim, as now defined, is to assess standards, not by testing every individual in the nation but by continuous, light sampling. No school would be visited more than once in every ten years or so, and even then individual pupils might be tested in different skills or areas of experience. Since the content of these tests would be unknown in advance, it would be impossible for a teacher to teach towards them. Nor would there be much point in holding oneself in readiness for a period that might turn out to be as long as a decade. Because of the methods of sampling, A.P.U. testing would be sufficiently intensive to provide an accurate picture of national standards and an indication of how those were changing over time.

The other main innovation of the A.P.U. is that it will be assessing not individual subjects but performance in most of the main areas of experience proposed by H.M.I.s as a basis for curriculum construction. (See above p. 128 *et seq.*) In the case of the A.P.U. these are: language, mathematics and science; and physical, ethical and aesthetic development. The first, fairly conventional, maths sampling began in 1978. Testing of investigative and 'creative' thought in maths should be ready to start in 1979. The testing of language, also beginning in 1979, is to include writing of every kind, from factual accounts of things already learnt, to a personal response to pictures, poetry or music. Reading tests will range from reading for information or the evaluation of a writer's viewpoint, to undirected reading for enjoyment. Testing in science will range across the curriculum to assess such skills as observation, selection, explanation – even open-mindedness – wherever they are in evidence. Physical, aesthetic and ethical development will also be looked at right across the board, though how this will be done remains uncertain.

It seems at least reasonable to hope that this kind of testing may provide a much better measure of what is now being attempted in primary and secondary schools – particularly in comprehensives – than either national testing for minimum skills or such subject-based exams as G.C.E. or C.S.E. In this context, it was highly interesting to note that in preparatory papers for the Great Debate – and if only to ward off the possibility of anything worse – such bodies as the Association of Assistant Mistresses, the Assistant Masters Association, the N.U.T. and others, all indicated much greater enthusiasm for the A.P.U. than they had ever done before.

But before I give the impression that a solution to the problem of national monitoring is in sight, I should add that the difficulties facing the A.P.U. are as large as its own considerable ambitions.

The biggest of the difficulties is technical, but since it may at the worst invalidate the whole proceedings it will be as well at least to indicate its nature. The problem is item banking. This is a method of testing supposed to get round the difficulty which occurs when tests go out of date and by doing so destroy the basis for comparability from one year to another. This is one of the greatest bugbears in assessing standards. (If, for example, the vocabulary in a reading test goes out of fashion, scores in later years will be artificially depressed. This is one of the factors that complicated the 1971 N.F.E.R. reading tests.) Item banking, on which the A.P.U. is likely to rely, involves collecting huge numbers of individual test-items all of properly measured 'difficulty value'. These are kept up to date with fresh items so that new and equally valid tests will pour continually from the bank. Though any pupil who is tested will take only a small sample of questions from the bank – the idea is that it will be possible to build up a national picture from the answers. But, as Harvey Goldstein and Steve Blinkhorn have pointed out,[75] for such a scheme to work it has to be shown that 'the order of difficulty of any set of items from the bank will be the same for all children'. Item banking, they say, has not yet reached this stage of development. Either the A.P.U. will have to modify its plans or its results will need to be 'viewed with circumspection' – a nicely judged understatement. This is a matter about which the A.P.U. is currently thinking deeply.

Other, possibly less substantial, difficulties over statistics have been mentioned.[76] The A.P.U., it is said, is being made to go too fast for political reasons; the results may be too subjective; and the press may seize with simple-minded, over-simplifying glee on any evidence of failure. Some experts even feel that the A.P.U., for all its intentions, will not be able to avoid having an impact on the curriculum. In an article in *The Times Educational Supplement*,[77] Professor Jack Wrigley of Reading University observed that 'when we measure comprehensively and accurately what we think is important then it becomes even more important'. This led him to conclude that the next round of curriculum development in Britain might well originate with the A.P.U. The biggest fear of all in the educational world is that interventionist governments of the future might use the machinery of the A.P.U. to introduce national testing designed on purpose to control the curriculum.

V: The teachers

There is no point in talking about standards without considering the teachers. Their education and training was one of the four main topics of the regional conferences and it is a most important one. But before embarking on it, it seems sensible to look, briefly, at who the teachers are, what attitudes they hold and how they are organized. This is because misunderstandings and false impressions about the teachers are legion.

There are just under 500,000 of them in England and Wales (467,829 in January 1977), and they and their pupils know something which most of the rest of us have forgotten – that by far the most important thing about school is the way it goes on day after day after day after day. The visitor may dart in, make a quick assessment, possibly, if he is foolish, offer his advice. And then he is off again, leaving teachers and pupils in the customary consciousness that they are locked together till the end of term. One must start therefore by doffing one's cap to them. Teachers also work a slightly longer week than most – $46\frac{1}{2}$ hours on average for secondary teachers, four of them at the week-end, compared to a national average of just over forty.[78] Less-experienced teachers put in fifty hours to stay abreast of the demands made on them.[79] This work is often extremely tiring. A recent N.A.S./U.W.T. survey[80] purported to show that deaths among male teachers approaching the end of their career had more than doubled in the past ten years. The number qualifying for a pension because of breakdown had more than trebled. Terry Casey, the union's general secretary, opined in his foreword that this was to do with reorganization, the size of schools and the difficulty of managing them. But even if matters are getting worse, as the N.A.S./U.W.T. believe, teachers in fact live a long time. The latest report from the Office of Population Censuses and Surveys[81] shows that they have one of the lowest death-rates of all occupational groups. And they have enviably long holidays.

Only a handful of teachers, as we saw in Chapter Three, are

radical to the point of holding revolutionary theories. At one meeting which I attended in 1977 there was talk of the extent to which governing bodies could be used as agencies for subversion; but that is a genuine rarity for a reporter's notebook. The best information on the profession as a whole comes from an N.O.P. poll conducted for *The Times Educational Supplement* in 1977,[82] repeating questions previously asked in 1974. This gave a strong impression of a comfortably established body of men and women. Far more of them (77 per cent) owned their own homes than in the population at large (53 per cent). Far more owned their own cars (81 per cent, as against 56 per cent). They had bank accounts (93 per cent) and unit trusts (13 per cent) and stocks and shares (11 per cent). They enjoyed going to the theatre and playing badminton. At the time of the survey more than half had been in their posts for the past five years (this compared interestingly with 1972 when 81 per cent had moved within the previous five years). Most interestingly of all, 34 per cent of them intended to vote Conservative, and 25 per cent for Labour. Compared to actual voting in the 1974 election this was a 2 per cent gain for the Conservatives, a 3 per cent loss for Labour. Meanwhile the 'don't-knows' had increased from 3 to 14 per cent. Conservative voting intentions were far more marked in primary schools, where women most heavily outnumber men. This tends to confirm the observation that in a profession where the majority are women – 58 per cent in the *T.E.S.* survey – there is a strong middle-class bias among women entrants.[83] The picture was one of a profession that was generally conservative with a small 'c'. The teachers in the *T.E.S.* survey were opposed by a large majority to the elimination of grammar schools and corporal punishment. They were opposed to 'pupil power' and 'parent power'. They also showed some enthusiasm for national testing at fourteen (62 per cent). This last, however, may well have been a misleading answer, partly suggested by the wording of the question; for teachers were strongly against a uniform curriculum, which would be one of the probable consequences of such testing. This raised the possibility, as Fred Jarvis, general secretary of the N.U.T.

pointed out, that teachers were in favour of national tests only so long as they ignored the obstacles. One particularly significant finding, of a less traditionalist kind, was that innovations in teaching method were reckoned to have done more good than harm. (Fifty-six per cent disagreed with the contrary proposition and 17 per cent did not know, leaving only 27 per cent who were critical of the effect of the new methods.) This might well suggest that the majority believed these methods were the best hope for the least able.

All-in-all, we may see the teachers as broadly representative of the conservative bourgeoisie, though prepared in some respects to follow their own convictions. In terms of attitudes there is one other, highly important aspect of the teacher force. This is recorded by Morrison and McIntyre in their book *Teachers and Teaching*:[84]

Of the many personal characteristics of teachers which have been studied, it is their *values* which most distinguish them. With a fair degree of consistency, those choosing teaching as a career have been found to be more 'people-oriented' in their values than most other occupational groups, placing emphasis on personal relationships, 'helping other people' and 'working with people'. Teachers tend to put correspondingly less value on what is seen as useful, efficient, economic.

One paradoxical consequence of this concern for their fellow human beings is that teachers tend to rate the self-development of pupils more highly than do the parents and, particularly, the children. For children and their families, career prospects come first by a long way.[85] This conflict of objectives *may* just mean that teachers take a longer view and think that pupils who have made the most of developing their personalities and aptitudes will be more flexible and better adapted to an uncertain future. But it probably also owes a lot to the teachers' traditional distaste for industry. Here too, however, one must enter a caveat. The N.U.T. has for a long time taken an interest, an official interest at least, in links between school and work. The Great Debate may have reinforced this and even altered teachers' attitudes, for the *T.E.S.* survey found that three-quarters of all teachers favoured more careers education, and two-thirds thought that the needs of industry and commerce deserved more consideration than they got at present.

Another point about attitudes is also worth noting here. This is that many teachers, though basically lovers of people rather than of machines, can have too much of a good thing. They are coming increasingly to feel that families are simply turning their own problems over to the schools, demanding that the schools inculcate higher standards of ethics and behaviour than are practised at home and blaming the schools when the children carry on as before. In this way, they believe, teachers are made the scapegoats for all the failings of society. Sir Alex Smith captured these feelings in an address to the N.U.T.'s National Education Conference in January 1977:[86]

It isn't the schools that create the difficult and inadequate housing conditions; it isn't the schools that generate indiscipline, discourtesy and lack of respect for law and order; it isn't the schools that generate the tidal wave of low standards that are blatantly disfiguring the centre of London and most cities . . .

N.A.S. speakers at the regional conferences took an even fiercer line. My notebooks are peppered with such remarks as this (from London):

The blame [for lack of motivation] should be thrown straight back on the parents because they are responsible for the attitudes I sometimes meet . . . They have failed their children and failed society . . . Let us assess those parents and put social pressure on them . . .

It is possible to interpret statements like these, even though they sound so angry, as a cry for help from a profession whose goodwill has been abused.

In terms of the organizations which represent them, the teachers are somewhat unusual. Headmasters, grammar school teachers and former grammar school teachers tend to belong to small, worthy and generally uncontroversial unions and associations. But the great mass of teachers, including a number of headmasters and headmistresses, belong to the National Union of Teachers (some 230,000 plus in 1977) and the National Association of Schoolmasters/Union of Women Teachers (about 100,000 in 1977). Both have already been mentioned frequently; and both pursue aims that are mutually contradictory. On the one hand, they want professional status and even self-regulation for their members, an aim which usually goes with decorous outward behaviour and attempts to restrict entry to the profession. On the other hand, they want to function as trades unions with plenty of industrial muscle. This leads them, and particularly the N.U.T., into a good deal of threatening talk which often seems to contain the ungracious and unpopular sentiment, 'Give us what we want – for the children's sake'. But industrial action itself is comparatively rare. When it does occur, however – and again, most particularly in the case of the N.U.T. – it is sometimes highly effective. (I shall deal in a moment with N.U.T. resistance to staffing cuts during the economic crisis of the mid-1970s.) But on one matter – the pursuit of a large membership – they behave with unabashed trade union zeal. This brings them into frequent collision with one another.

Meetings of the Schools Council have often been enlivened by quarrelling over the rights and wrongs of their comparative representation. This animosity reached such a pitch in the autumn of 1977 that the N.U.T. at one point declined to attend an important series of meetings with Shirley Williams because it was not allowed to send along two more representatives than it had previously done. The union only agreed to start coming again when A.C.A.S., the Advisory Conciliation and Arbitration Service, was called in. In another, even more comical dispute, trainee teachers at a polytechnic decided to allow only N.U.T. representatives to recruit among their number. In reprisal, the N.A.S. threatened to prevent them from doing teaching practice in the schools. In matters like this, both unions sometimes seem prepared to go out of their way to spoil their own chances of being thought professional. The quarrel is particularly important at secondary level. Here the two unions are now of about equal strength and the N.A.S./U.W.T. is determined to exact full recognition for itself.

The differences between the N.U.T. and the N.A.S. are, however, at least as great as their similarities. The N.U.T. is basically a liberal organization leading its members from well to the left of their centre. (This was illustrated by the *T.E.S.* poll which showed that a vast majority of all teachers wanted to keep the grammar schools. The grammar vote was strongest in primary schools where N.U.T. members are thickest on the ground. Yet the N.U.T. itself is strongly in favour of comprehensives.) But the N.U.T. members do seem more inclined than N.A.S. members to the optimistic interpretation of life that so often goes with a liberal approach to teaching. This can be seen by comparison between the *T.E.S.* poll, which included all teacher unions and hence a majority of N.U.T. members, and a recent N.A.S./U.W.T. poll[87] to which few N.U.T. members responded. Taking the whole teacher force (the *T.E.S.* survey), most felt that standards had risen (24 per cent) or stayed the same (32 per cent). A minority of 36 per cent felt that they had fallen. The N.A.S. survey showed a dramatically different position. Fifty-four per cent felt that academic standards had fallen in the past ten years. Sixty-five per cent believed that 'general standards' had fallen.

The poor overall response to the N.A.S. survey (a meagre 48 per cent) illustrates another difference between the two organizations. For while the N.U.T. is famous for the solidity of its research findings, this is not so clearly the case with the N.A.S. Indeed the N.A.S., with its rather strident line on discipline, has often been regarded, perhaps somewhat unfairly, as vocal but unimportant. Now the rightward swing of the pendulum has recently brought it nearer the centre of educational politics. During the Great Debate, when luminaries of the N.U.T. were denouncing the exercise as a charade and cooperating with visible reluctance, the N.A.S./U.W.T. made conspicuous attempts to contribute to policy formation. Some critics, exaggeratedly, now see the N.A.S. as being in alliance with the Department of Education. In fact, the N.U.T. remains far more important. Despite a current surplus of teachers, which should in theory have reduced the N.U.T.'s bargaining

power, its numbers mean that neither central government nor
local authorities can take the smallest step without at least considering how the teachers will react.

This account of the teachers and their unions has so far omitted an issue made prominent by Dr Rhodes Boyson and other
Black Paper writers – the level of education of the teachers
themselves. This is intimately bound up with the question of
teacher numbers and teacher training, both of which are in their
turn inextricably linked with the performance of the economy
and the level of government spending. It is to these topics that I
shall now turn, starting with the level of education among student teachers and ending with a thumb-nail sketch of the issues
that were discussed during the Great Debate.

The allegation of the pessimists is basically that the teachers
are inadequately educated and that quality is sacrificed to quantity during periods of expansion. The figures seem to suggest the
opposite.[88] Between 1957 and 1972 the number of places for
trainee teachers leapt from 27,000 to 117,000, with the biggest
increase coming in the last few years of the period. But throughout this time, the qualifications of trainee teachers improved.
After a slight decline in the immediate aftermath of the Second
World War, the percentage of graduates in both primary and
secondary schools has risen steadily. The number with no
qualification beyond 'O' level fell from 36 per cent in 1960 to 26
per cent in 1975. 'A' level results also improved.

The one area of serious and continuing failure is in mathematics. As Shirley Williams confirmed in January 1977, only
three fifths of non-graduate teachers who completed their training after 1967 had passed 'O' level maths. Since this was a period
of tremendous expansion, the result is that huge numbers of
teachers with little or no mathematics are now at work in the
schools. Because most of these teachers are young, they will be
around for a long time. Professor William Bonner, a member
of the National Council for Educational Standards – which is a
Black Paper offshoot – claimed in 1977 that nearly one third of
secondary school mathematics teaching was being done by
teachers without a degree in the subject or without maths as

the specialism of their teaching certificate. Nearly half the children in primary schools were taught by teachers without 'O' level maths, he said. The government itself was prepared to admit, on the basis of calculations generally criticized as over-optimistic, to a shortage of 2000 graduate maths teachers. (A D.E.S. staffing survey, underway as I write, should soon yield a more accurate picture.)

There are also teacher shortages in the craft subjects and, to a lesser extent now, in physics. But this is not quite the end of the story, for even though qualifications and numbers in other subjects appear generally all right on paper, there remains a strong feeling both among administrators and among the teachers themselves that many rather weak individuals were admitted to the profession during the most recent bout of expansion (the late 1960s and early 1970s). Morrison and McIntyre[89] stated in 1973 that because of the teacher shortage of that time, 'the great majority of applicants with the minimum necessary qualifications have been admitted to professional training courses, the failure rate has been very low (less than 2 per cent on average), and few qualified teachers have had any difficulty getting jobs'. The authors of the Yellow Paper showed that they shared some of the same worries when they remarked that today's teachers were, on average, somewhat less impressive than the grammar school teachers of yore. Even Sir Ronald Gould, former general secretary of the N.U.T. and a strong defender of the teachers, lamented in a speech in 1977 that pressure had been put on colleges to pass teachers whom they thought unfit. Then he went on: 'Let us be honest about this: the Department [of Education and Science] cared nothing for quality when there were not enough teachers.' So it is not just the Black Paper writers who have their doubts about the calibre of some of our teachers.

The main result of the great increase in teacher-training places was that the supply of teachers kept up with and even slightly exceeded the growth in the school population (and this despite the artificial boost created by the raising of the school leaving age). Teacher–pupil ratios have fallen steadily and gratifyingly ever since the Second World War. In 1946, in primary schools, the ratio was 1:30; in secondary schools 1:21·7. In January 1976 it was 1:23·9 in primary schools and 1:17 in secondary schools. Improvement in teacher–pupil ratios has been one of the main aims of the teacher unions and its advantages seem obvious. Surprisingly, however, work by several researchers has shown that, so far as ordinary-sized classes are concerned, the addition of a few more pupils makes no difference to the speed with which children learn to read. But teachers believe that smaller groups do make all the difference in atmosphere and behaviour and the mere fact that they find small classes easier is itself a reason for working to improve ratios. Teacher–pupil ratios are, however, somewhat misleading. In very many cases not just primary but also secondary classes still contain more than 30 pupils. This is partly a matter of organization (many 'A' level groups are tiny) and partly because there is an increasing tendency for teachers not to teach. Administration absorbs more and more of them. Often in an infant or junior school with a staff of only nine or ten, the head does no teaching at all; in secondary schools, the number and the proportion involved in administration is surprisingly large. A school may retain a non-teaching head and several non-teaching deputies or other high-ranking staff. They devise exceedingly complicated charts and send out large numbers of pieces of paper full of complicated instructions. Comprehensive reorganization brought many closet bureaucrats out into the open. But the biggest growth by far in the number of non-teaching teachers flows from the increase in 'pastoral care'. This is a large-scale attempt by schools, often the bigger ones, to overcome impersonality of atmosphere by providing far more individual advice (often described, to lend it dignity, as 'counselling'). This is done because the teachers care about the children, but it has had the effect of mopping up much of the improvement in teacher–pupil ratios. Growth in pastoral arrangements, as the H.M.I.s observed in one of the York papers, had brought the danger that 'from a previous situation in which academic considerations predominated there may have been too big a swing in the opposite direction with proper social goals pursued to an extent and in ways which can put academic standards at a discount'. (This is a good example of the curiously lulling language used by the inspectorate. It allows them to be rude without any noticeable change in tone.)

So far as the teacher unions were concerned the answer to this and almost every other problem was more and more growth in the number of teachers. But during the 1970s two things occurred that totally undermined this programme. The first was the enormous drop in the birth-rate already alluded to. This meant that far fewer teachers would be required and it seemed likely at some future date to threaten even the jobs of those already at work. The second, which compounded the consequences of the falling birth-rate, was the economic crisis of 1974 and the next three years.

To understand the way in which this worked through the educational system, it is necessary to grasp a peculiarity of educational financing. Though education is administered by the local authorities and takes up about two-thirds of their budget, most of the money comes from central government in the form of the rate support grant. This is calculated, in a bewildering manner understood by few, to some extent in accordance with need. The government puts in so much for teachers and so much for materials, so much for this and so much for that. But the local authorities are allowed to use it just as they think fit and may even, if they wish, divert it to paying for the roads or any other of their services. Following the 1974 oil crisis, the government began to reduce public spending. In education, the principal victims were outside the mandatory years of schooling, mainly nursery and adult education. Both of these have sustained what seems likely to be permanent damage. In respect of the mandatory years, the government claimed that teacher ratios would not suffer because enough money had been included in the rate support grant to pay existing teachers. But something quite different transpired, and from 1975 onwards, because teacher–pupil ratios were no longer improving as had once been planned, thousands of newly qualified teachers found themselves without work each autumn. Most, in the end, abandoned all hope of teaching. And many of the rural counties, whose share of the rate support grant had been reduced so as to favour the cities, claimed that the only way they could make the cuts the government demanded was by reducing the number of teachers. There just was not enough in the rate support kitty, they said, to pay the teachers they already had. So in addition to the thousands of young teachers without work, existing teaching posts were threatened up and down the country.

In these circumstances, the N.U.T.'s left-wing Rank and File movement wanted full-tilt industrial action. The N.U.T. leadership easily outflanked them, going instead for selective action wherever staffing cuts were proposed or classes exceptionally large. The idea was that this would seem reasonable to the broad mass of their membership and might even command public support. In this way, despite the great difficulty of protecting jobs in a declining labour market, some 3000 jobs were, in the end, saved. Many other local authorities were probably deterred from reducing the number of teachers. Up to 1978 at least, ratios were maintained. But for the unemployed young teachers there was little anyone could do. The government's readiness to abandon them contrasted depressingly with the history of Concorde. The original misjudgement over Concorde was followed by more and more spending in an attempt to make good the original losses, regardless of the environmental impact of the aeroplane. But the investment in the training of these young teachers, whose services might actually be of public benefit, was sacrificed without prolonged debate. Teachers, it seemed, were better candidates for unemployment than workers in the aero industry.

The D.E.S. had known about the fall in birth-rate in 1972 and had at that time considered, secretly, a reduction in the number of places in teacher training colleges[90] but there was little evidence then to suggest the birth-rate would continue at its new, low level. But now the oil crisis and a continuing dearth of future school children meant that estimates of the number of initial training places needed at the end of the decade had to be revised down and down from the peak of 117,000 to just 35,000.

Ten thousand places were to be set aside for in-service training. (This, if it happens, will be a ten-fold increase.) But even taking the number down to 45,000 involved what are probably the most swingeing cuts ever yet seen in education; and in terms of lost opportunities, the burden will fall most heavily on women.

Colleges and departments of education used to come in three main shapes. Some, mostly the oldest, were simple teacher training colleges, often in the country, frequently isolated. Others were in polytechnics. Others again were attached to universities, and mostly known as Institutes of Education. These last tended to provide one-year courses for graduates. The polytechnics and the specialist training colleges – sometimes called monotechnics – laid on three-year, certificate courses for non-graduates. Academic studies went hand in hand with the theory and practice of teaching. This was the so-called 'concurrent' pattern. But in 1972 the James Report on teacher training[91] advocated a different approach. The trouble with concurrent training, James said, was that it locked young people into teaching earlier than necessary. He recommended that after studying their academic subject for two years, students should have an option between going on to a straightforward academic degree or doing the professional side of teacher training (in a 'consecutive' pattern). The first part of courses designed on this principle would lead to a new qualification, the Diploma in Higher Education (Dip. H.E.), which was intended either to stand in its own right or to function as a building block in a four-year-degree course. For those who wanted to be teachers, the Dip. H.E. would be followed by two years of professional training, at the end of which a degree would be awarded. In this way, the prestige of the initial academic subject would be enhanced (because it was part of a course leading to a degree) and all newly qualifying teachers, whether educated à la James or in the older pattern of three years' degree-course plus one of training, would be graduates of similar educational status. The three-year certificate would be phased out. Another idea was to bring education students into the mainstream of higher education by somehow ending the isolation of the 'monotechnic' colleges.

The D.E.S. seems to have borne James much in mind while cutting down the number of teacher training places. Isolation was ended in many cases by the simple expedient of closing down colleges. Some of the remainder were merged with universities and some with polytechnics. Others were thrown together or with colleges of further education to create, almost accidentally, a quite new type of animal known as an Institute of Higher Education. Many of these new colleges and departments began to offer degree courses, usually in the arts subjects and often starting with a Dip. H.E. In some cases the student had the possibility of converting half-way through to teacher training. The future teachers were able to study in a rather more open society, gaining some flexibility for themselves. From the government's point of view the arrangement was a neat one, since at least some of the former teacher training colleges and departments were kept alive by the new courses but would be able to expand their teacher training once again if either the economy or the birth-rate should happen to turn up. By early 1978, the National Union of Students, another body with a reputation for good homework, was already warning of a possible teacher shortage in the 1990s. But under the new arrangements, even if the N.U.S. were right, the government could hope to cope with less disruption than last time round. Meanwhile arrangements were made to end the old, three-year certificate. By 1982, it was hoped, all new teachers would be graduates.

In this way many of the James recommendations slowly came to be adopted and a somewhat more rational pattern began to emerge. But the cost was high. Over-expansion followed by swift contraction meant disaster for many institutions and thousands upon thousands of individuals. There was much anxiety about the standard of the new degree courses, particularly where these were validated by universities. (The Council for National Academic Awards, the validating body for the polytechnics, was much more cautious about the courses it approved.) Nor did the pattern of closures seem to have taken much account of the success or failure of the individual colleges in their work of training teachers. Looked at overall, the policy appears, as happens so often in education, to have been dictated as much by administrative as educational objectives.

Debate over what should actually be taught in teacher training colleges took place, accordingly, while the colleges themselves were in the greatest disarray. The colleges came in for a battering. There is no section of the educational world so frequently abused by the rest of its inhabitants. Here, to give the reader something of the flavour, are one or two remarks made by Kay Wareham, in her presidential address to the annual conference of the Association of Career Teachers in 1977:

Every year I have students in my classroom on school practice, and every year I am appalled at the inadequate preparation they receive before being sent into the classroom.

Over the years I have noticed a steady deterioration in the standards of both students and their tutors. I see inadequate lesson notes and preparation, spelling mistakes on the blackboard, bad grammar and poor diction when talking to the class, and scanty or non-existent visual aids which would never have been tolerated when I was in training...

Standards have suffered at the hands of the reformists, many of whom have gone all out for new and untried methods simply because they are different.

The notion of continually declining standards often depends, as we have seen, on the temperament of the speaker. But the idea of students poorly prepared for the classroom is very prevalent. In their initial training, students commonly have to fit in not just classroom techniques, but the academic subjects they will teach, as well as courses on psychology, sociology and philosophy, often of a rather speculative nature. Some observers, like Devlin and Warnock,[92] want less of the latter and a great deal more concentration on classroom craft, making use of simulated teaching practice and of tapes and films that would offer a chance for reflection on how to deal with classroom crises. This kind of down-to-earth approach, which would inevitably involve more contact between school and college, would help to close the enormous gap that has opened out between the two sectors. This gap was often mentioned during the Great Debate and college lecturers were heavily criticized for being, allegedly, out of touch.

Another idea stressed particularly by conservatives was the critical role of discipline. What young teachers needed above all, they said, was knowledge of how to obtain control and keep it. This was often proposed as if it were a new idea. In fact, the imparting of this skill was one of the main aims of teacher training in the nineteenth century and the earlier part of this. Historically, it was replaced little by little by an approach which laid more emphasis on human understanding and a supposedly enlightened attitude to education. In this context it is clear that what people are calling for today is not something new but a reverse swing of the pendulum in training colleges as well as schools. And here, as much as in the schools, there is a risk that it could swing too far.

It is in-service training, however, rather than initial training which has emerged as the main subject of debate. The authors of the James Report envisaged a three-stage process of teacher training. Initial studies would be followed by a period of induction and this would be followed by regular in-service topping-up. Tentative moves have been made towards a worthwhile induction scheme, in which young teachers would have the sympathetic support of teacher-tutors and time off for special courses. So far, all that has actually happened are pilot schemes in Liverpool and Sunderland. In-service training for the fully qualified, though absolutely vital for the improvement of a static teacher force, has prospered even less. One reason is that the moment anyone begins to discuss what should be taught, abstractions take over from reality. The school curriculum is a topic that brings out the worst in teachers. The subject of a curriculum for the teachers themselves brings out the very worst.[93] Another reason is argument over the control and staffing of in-service courses. The National Association of Teachers in Further and Higher Education, which represents the college lecturers, wants to see as much as possible of this training concentrated in the colleges. The N.U.T. would like to see it based on the schools, with teachers in charge (and more teachers, naturally, to stand in for the teachers who were occupied with courses). The country also possesses some 500 Teachers Centres, set up originally by local authorities but under teacher control and intended mainly as bases for curriculum development. Now that that innovation is not so fashionable they are looking for a new mission. In-service training seems a very natural one.

None of these difficulties and disagreements compares with the trouble over money. The government claimed in 1976 that it had set aside seven million pounds for in-service training under the rate support grant. To everybody's chagrin and nobody's surprise, the local authorities diverted the bulk of this money in other directions. Despite the many fine words being spoken, in-service training continued to decline as an indirect result of central-government economies. Shirley Williams at this point began to give serious consideration, as other education secretaries had done, to the idea of making a specific grant for in-service training, so that money for this at least could not be spirited away. This change would have involved a major shift of policy. For the local authorities stoutly defend the principle of being allowed to spend the rate support grant any way they want. Education is the only major area of social policy in which the responsible ministry cannot finance its own projects, and the authorities want to keep it that way. Mrs Williams thought in-service training so important that she was willing to brave their anger. But she was overruled by cabinet colleagues arguing in the name of local autonomy. The case for not making the change was amplified in an interesting leader in *The Times Educational Supplement*.[94] If the local authorities knew they could get money by neglecting particular educational services, argued the *T.E.S.*, then they would be under a strong temptation to do so. The government would wade in deeper and deeper, gradually becoming a general paymaster and so accruing power to itself even if it didn't mean to. All innovation would pass from local to central government.

The arguments about in-service training (which is often known, in a world of acronyms, as INSET) were concerned with helping those teachers still within reach of help. There was also a good deal of worry over teachers who were beyond the pale, genuine incompetents holding down undeserved jobs. There have always been bad teachers and miserable schools. Lady Plowden, discussing events in the ten years since the publication of her report, recalled that in a survey of all primary schools done by H.M.I.s in 1964–5 twenty-eight schools (out of 20,000) were categorized as being 'a bad school where children suffer from laziness, indifference, gross incompetence or unkindness on the part of the staff'. It would be surprising if there were no schools like this today. The accusations in the William Tyndale affair brought all these worries up to the surface.

The position of head-teachers also caused concern. Once chosen, often after brief and undemanding interviews, they were able to wield virtually despotic powers until retirement age. Many were admirable, a few were deeply dreadful. What could be done about them?

Yet another problem, perhaps a more profound one, surfaced from time to time and was allowed to go away again. It is difficult to put simply, but I shall try. Since the ending of the psychological era, sociology has preoccupied teachers more and more. It is taught increasingly in the training colleges. If there is one simple message in the sociology of education, it is that working-class children and children from unsupportive backgrounds do not do as well at school as children of the same ability who come from helpful and/or middle-class backgrounds. By an almost universal and tragic misunderstanding, new work in linguistics is also taken to mean that working-class children are at an insuperable disadvantage. No force within the teachers' power seems strong enough to put this right. The resultant pessimism means that teachers are inclined to expect even less than before from working-class children. Yet teachers' expectations have been shown to be one of the most potent factors in raising children's standard of performance. Peter Newsam sometimes tells I.L.E.A. staff that the single most important thing that could happen in education today would be for teachers to raise their expectations.

VI: Who should control the schools?

Most of the anxiety before, during and after the Great Debate has revolved around two questions: how to raise standards and how to bring school and the 'world of work' a little closer. But underlying the public discussion, there has been one other major unresolved theme: the question of who should hold the power. For if one wishes to raise standards or to shift the direction of the schools, it is necessary first to have control, or to exercise a powerful influence over such basics as the curriculum, discipline, the appointment of staff, the future of incompetent teachers and, of course, finance. Quite logically, properly even, the period of the Great Debate has been one during which most of the main interests have battled for a greater measure of control. The principal contestants have been the teachers, represented by their unions, and the government, as represented by prime minister, secretary of state for education, D.E.S. and Inspectorate. The Taylor Committee on school governors was in the meantime gathering evidence, writing its report and clearly preparing to take the lists as champion of parents and 'community'. Only the local authorities, despite their vital interest in the matter, refrained from making any obvious power-play. This section discusses some of the moves in the game and a few of the considerations that would be involved in any redistribution of power.

At the time when the game began – let us say, for the sake of argument, when Fred Mulley and James Callaghan conferred in 1976 – both the government and the teachers had considerable powers and were steadily enlarging them. The government controlled capital expenditure on the schools and broadly set the level for current spending. Though the local authorities retained the power to foil the government in some particulars of spending, no power in the educational world could stop the government fron economizing when it wanted to, as it did from 1975 onwards. Local authorities, lecturers and students all tried in various ways and failed. As is well known, the power of the paymaster increases when cash is in short supply and this was the position in which the government now found itself. Equally important, the government had little by little taken to itself the power to say what kind of schools the local authorities should provide. This was not the intention of the 1944 Act. Explaining its purpose when it was before the House of Commons, R. A. Butler, as President of the Board of Education, had been quite clear. 'The local education authority', he said, 'will have the responsibility for the broad type of education given in the ... school ... and its place in the local system ...'[95] Mr Crosland undermined this, by administrative fiat, with his 'comprehensivizing' circular of 1965.

When administrative measures finally failed to do the trick, the government brought in the 1976 Education Act and so reversed the Butler principle. This was a major shift of power away from the local authorities and into the hands of central government.

Through its ability to accept or reject comprehensive schemes the government had also come to exercise detailed administrative power over local school structures. (Mrs Thatcher's administration was very active here, intervening frequently to preserve individual grammar schools.) And though most teacher training was theoretically in the hands of the local authorities, the government had itself been entirely responsible, first for building up the colleges, then for suddenly knocking them down again. The government also had the power to decide on the qualifications of teachers, and the power to authorize public examinations. The exercise of this last-mentioned power is now emerging as one of the most controversial aspects of debate; and this, of course, is because of the great extent to which exams determine the secondary curriculum.

What the government lacked, however, was direct power over the curriculum. In theory, both as defined by Butler in his House of Commons speech and as written into the 1945 model articles of governance,[96] broad responsibility lay with the education authority. The model articles said it was the authority's business to 'determine the general educational character of the school...'. But 'subject thereto the Governors shall have the general direction of the conduct and curriculum of the school'. In practice the local authorities have great influence over the general tenor of a school. Good administration is a powerful stimulus to performance. Local authority inspectorates, if they are good, may also wield an influence over syllabus content and teaching method. But this stops far short of control of the curriculum. The governors, despite the powers theoretically delegated to them by the authorities, have even less control. (Their present, and potential, role will be discussed a little later.) The primary curriculum is almost entirely in the hands of head teachers, subject only to such restraints as lack of money or the kind of community served. In secondary schools the exam system means that the universities, the exam boards and the entry qualifications for various occupations have a very great impact. But the rest, effectively, is up to the head. As the Taylor Report said (in paragraph 2.2.): 'Heads invariably maintained that they were entirely responsible for deciding what was taught...'. This is why we have our present fragmented curriculum.

A Conservative government, with Sir David Eccles as minister in charge, tried to intervene in 1960 by setting up a curriculum study group. He was beaten off by the teachers, and his study group replaced by the Schools Council. This conformed to the prevailing ideology of the time by having teachers in control at every critical point. But the Schools Council was intended only as a centre for curriculum development and research, not as a body that would plan a national curriculum. It operated on the 'cafeteria principle' – I have stolen the phrase from Denis Lawton, professor of curriculum studies at London University's Institute of Education. Various courses were worked out and put on offer, and teachers were free to pick the ones they wanted. On the exam front, too, the teachers tried to seize power not so as to impose a system of their own but so as to enlarge the freedom of individual schools to do more nearly what they wanted. One of the critical principles of C.S.E., and one that has probably introduced into the curriculum both more rubbish and more visionary teaching than anything else, is that C.S.E. boards have to examine any Mode III syllabus submitted to them by a school provided only that it is examinable and correctly labelled. There is, in other words, no mechanism of accountability in Mode III exams at sixteen-plus. At eighteen-plus the teachers now wanted freedom from what Dr Patrick Nuttgens, director of Leeds Polytechnic, recently called 'the stranglehold' of the universities. The Schools Council, with its schemes for sixteen-plus reform, for C.E.E. and 'N' and 'F' had become the advance guard of the teacher army, aiming for control over every phase of examinations and so, finally, of the whole curriculum.

The 1944 Act had made the government responsible in law for 'the promotion of the education of the people of England and Wales'. What seems to have happened in 1976 is that worry over standards, coinciding with the teachers' run for freedom through the sixteen-plus proposals, made the government more than usually mindful of that duty. The response was to seek a yet greater enlargement of central power. The Yellow Paper of 1976 advocated it. Mr Callaghan carried the process further, though carefully avoiding confrontation with the teachers. The regional conferences were yet another extension. The D.E.S. had previously had great success in influencing the curriculum through committees of inquiry – the Plowden and Bullock reports are good examples. Now it put its worries on the public agenda through its series of carefully orchestrated mock debates. This was an exercise in seizing the initiative which created a great deal of kerfuffle but was not necessarily a better way of doing things.[97]

Both the Yellow Paper and Mr Callaghan in his Ruskin speech raised the spectre of a centrally imposed, core curriculum. This, it soon turned out, was never likely to materialize. A letter from Shirley Williams to the Taylor Committee on 5 November 1976 gave this undertaking:

There is no question of the government contemplating the introduction of a detailed central control of the school curriculum which would deny teachers reasonable flexibility or diminish the contribution which local education authorities and the managers or governors should make to the conduct of the schools.[98]

An imposed core would have been politically impossible. Nevertheless, the government appeared to be seeking more influence. There was plenty of room for manoeuvre in the phrase 'reasonable flexibility'. Ministers who attended the regional conferences paid great attention to those speakers who complained that differences in teaching and curriculum from school to school made it extremely difficult for families to move about the country. One or two people mentioned this, for instance, at the Exeter conference. They included a general who spoke of the difficulties facing army personnel. Later Gordon Oakes, the junior minister in charge that day, singled this out in his press conference as one of the most important messages received. But since the 'message' occupied only a couple of minutes of discussion time, it was clear to observers not only which way the wind was blowing but also, equally clear whence. Continuity of curriculum, and the equality of opportunity implied by this, became a major governmental theme.

Her Majesty's Inspectors also intervened in the question of the curriculum. To understand the significance of this it is again necessary to go back a little. The Inspectorate has been in business now for over one hundred years. In the days of payment by results, it used to be a fearsome instrument of control, though even then, as Matthew Arnold's writings indicate, there was some feeling that more might be achieved by advice and consent than by authoritarian 'telling'. Nevertheless, the inspectors inspected and produced written reports on the schools they visited. But there were never quite enough H.M.I.s. During the 1930s, they visited only about 15 per cent of maintained secondary schools each year (and there were, of course, very few of these at the time). After the Second World War there was a slight resurgence of inspection, though this concentrated mainly on the grammar schools. During the 1950s and 1960s, inspections dwindled fairly sharply. More and more emphasis was placed on the friendly and consultative, rather than the numinous, role. In 1968 a Select Committee report finally ended cyclical inspections. Inspections continue where schools are in trouble, or where a school is studied because it is either representative or particularly promising.[99] But there are today only about 300 H.M.I.s available for this work, out of a total of some 450. Without major remodelling of the service, it is clearly out of the question to think of starting up regular inspections again. Their abandonment, however, has provoked the bitter resentment of educational conservatives. When these denounce the Inspectorate, which they do quite frequently, this is one of the reasons. Another is the belief that the Inspectorate have uncritically endorsed new fashions merely because they were fashionable. There is a little truth in this as regards Her Majesty's Inspectorate and probably a good deal as regards the entirely separate inspectors – often known, significantly, as advisers – employed by the education authorities.

Since the ending of inspections, the H.M.I.s have carved out a new role for themselves. Sheila Browne, in making the main ex-cathedra pronouncement on the subject,[100] defined this as five-fold: keeping the Secretary of State up to date; maintaining an information service which presents facts and the interpretation of facts, including judgements, best guesses and sometimes speculation; the establishment of sound and useful working generalizations (though based on the scrutiny of particular cases); frankness and independence; and 'the encouragement of good, and where necessary, better education'.

In trying to pursue these objectives the H.M.I.s had latterly worked through influence, exercised by a word here, a word there and friendly if sometimes inscrutable behaviour. At the time of the Great Debate, they emerged into the public arena, with a whole series of publications many of which have already been discussed. Subsequent publications include the primary survey and the secondary survey, in 1978 and 1979 respectively. These are likely to be critically important, providing real information and so a better basis than any we have at present for deciding policy. As we have seen, the inspectors have also begun to look at the curriculum in a way that would provide some coherence without detailed control. This approach is embodied in the work of the A.P.U. and the format of the secondary survey.

All of these activities, taken together, go some way towards justifying the Yellow Paper claim that the Inspectorate is 'without doubt the most powerful single agency to influence what goes on in schools, both in kind and standard'. If standards are now too low, the Inspectorate is partly to blame; if they are going to improve, the Inspectorate will have to be involved.

The government, then, was advancing on several fronts at once during 1976 and 1977. It possessed the power of the purse, was busily reorganizing the schools and had now put the curriculum, formerly the prerogative of the teachers, firmly on the public agenda. On one curricular flank the Inspectorate was advancing. On the other, by her exercise of the veto on exam proposals, the Secretary of State had the power to beat off the assault of the teachers. The teachers themselves, as Taylor continued to gather evidence, were now being taken in the rear by the parents. For a real possibility was emerging that the Taylor Committee would try to give the parents, who were likely to be an important element in the membership of redesigned governing bodies, a say in the curriculum and the other fundamentals.

In the partnership envisaged by those who framed the 1944 Education Act, the parents had been neglected. It was their duty in law to send their children to school, but they received in exchange no control whatsoever of the system, nor even any right to information. Participation could only be achieved through local or parliamentary elections; and elections, except on very rare occasions, are decided on other issues. The Act seemed to suggest that local authorities would have to consider the wishes of parents over which school their children should attend. This right was effectively denied by the small print. (It is only recently that parents have begun to defy local authorities on any large scale, discovering as they did so that by going right through all the processes of appeal they could generally get their way. The topic is discussed in Chapter One. But this is very hard on children since it embroils them in a battle and keeps them out of school. For most, therefore, it is not a realistic option. Parents have little choice.) As matters developed under the 1944 Act, governing bodies were virtually powerless and were anyway composed mostly of political nominees, appointments compromising to the party balance in the local education authority. If governors and managers had a function apart from attending to the fabric of the buildings, this was saying 'yes' to the headmaster and the local authority simultaneously. The intentions of the 1944 Act were totally ignored. All proceeded by mutual consent so long as the teachers had their way.[101]

During the 1960s this pattern began to change. Many Parent Teacher Associations (or P.T.A.s) were now formed and the best of these gave parents an opportunity to be involved, not just in fund-raising but also in educational discussions. Responding to the trend towards participation, many local authorities began to recruit parents, elected by other parents, on to their governing bodies. Pressure groups such as the Advisory Centre for Education (A.C.E.) and Confederation for the Advancement of State Education (C.A.S.E.) 'early saw governing bodies as one of the means by which they could achieve the ends they had set themselves'.[102] Late in the 1960s the National Association of Governors and Managers was formed specifically to revitalize school management and government. The issue became a topical one and more and more parents began to realize their lack of power over a system which exercised power over their children.

Another highly interesting development was the formation of community schools. The local authorities and teachers who promoted these thought they should be far more closely involved with the neighbourhood and all the people who wanted to use them – parents and other adults, as well as school-age children – than any schools had ever been before. The best known of these, as well as the most radical, is probably Countesthorpe in Leicestershire, but there are many others from Gwent to Birmingham and points more northerly. They represent a real attempt to bring school and community together.

All these developments, however positive, were strictly limited. P.T.A.s, as Taylor pointed out, needed the permission of the head. Sometimes this was not given. Often middle-class parents were over-represented. A Schools Council Research Project,[103] whose results were published while Taylor was at work, found that where this happened there was a tendency for working-class parents to withdraw, or even to become antagonistic to the school. P.T.A.s are therefore not ideal as the only link between schools and parents. So far as governing bodies are concerned, there seemed from a parental point of view not much point in having them at all unless they had greater powers. And even in the community schools, the community had few rights. The point was made by Stuart Maclure, editor of *The Times Educational Supplement*, in 1974;[104] 'So far, participation has been largely on the school's terms. However radically intentioned, the professional teacher's contribution has been dominant; it has been his pleasure to go out and find the community and drag it in . . . A good deal – I suspect most – of what now passes for community school activity is discreetly paternalistic . . .'

This means, in summary, that for parents the situation is still one in which there are many duties and few rights. What this can involve is easily demonstrated.

The schools keep records of children. Sometimes these records contain highly prejudicial statements which may, if they are inaccurate, unfairly damage a child's future either at his next school or when it comes to getting a job. Over the years, enormous resentment has built up about this among various pressure groups. The local authorities are, in the last resort, responsible for records and have so far mostly supported the teachers, who want to keep the records secret. The teachers use the perfectly plausible argument that if the records were available for scrutiny nothing of any moment would ever be written in them. And records, they say, are very useful in helping teachers to provide the best education for a child. But the point is – and it is partly this which so infuriates the pressure groups – that there is nothing the parents can do about it unless local authorities, out of the goodness of their hearts, decide to change the system.

Similarly, because there is no right even to general information, great abuses may be perpetrated. In June 1977 Shirley Williams issued a draft circular listing nineteen items of information she thought should 'normally be made available to parents'. (Note the word 'normally'.) These ranged from 'the basis on which places are normally allocated', to 'public examinations for which pupils are prepared, and the range of subjects and options available'. Perhaps Mrs Williams was being over-punctilious in listing such obvious things as these, but the fact that she even thought she had to do so indicates to me, as a parent of two children in maintained schools, a profoundly unsatisfactory state of affairs.

So what part should the parents play?

Taylor, reviewing the evidence, said that parents organizations had asked that governing bodies should both include more parents and have a say in drawing up the general educational aims of the schools. (On their visits to individual governing bodies, however, the Taylor Committee met 'a large number of parents and governors who did not question that they should defer to the headteacher on all educational matters'.) Witnesses 'representative of the communities and wider society served by the schools' also felt they should have some part in decisions about the curriculum. Local education authorities, on the contrary, felt that power over the curriculum should remain where it was. And so, of course, did the teachers' organizations.[105]

The Assistant Masters Association declared that the curriculum 'best falls within the competence of professionally trained, experienced and practising teachers'. The N.U.T., in their evidence, accepted that it was 'entirely natural and legitimate for the governors to be interested in the curriculum as part of its concern *to support school activities and to press for additional resources*'. (My italics. This wording is important because of the menial role it assigns to governors.) Then the N.U.T. continued, 'The distinction must however be maintained between interest and responsibility. In the context of the curriculum, the latter must unequivocally be given to the head-teacher and the staff.'

This, though couched in officialese, is a strong warning to trespassers. Some of the emotion behind it may be felt in the following paragraphs written by Max Morris. Mr Morris is a former president of the N.U.T., remains an influential member of the executive and perhaps the union's foremost teacher-spokesman. Schools, Mr Morris wrote,[106] belong to the local authorities who are accountable in a general sense to the electorate. The schools have certain duties towards the authorities, such as striving to their utmost for 'reasonable' standards of literacy and numeracy and for the 'highest standards of personal and interpersonal behaviour'. (His list was a much longer one than this.) They owe similar duties to the parents.

But what the public authorities cannot expect is the right to interfere in the day to day carrying out by the schools of their professional responsibilities. Teaching methods, syllabus planning and operation, curriculum development, discipline, the internal organization of the school, for example, are the teachers' jobs. No profession can work successfully if such matters were [sic] to be the subject of interference or indeed what one can only describe as 'amateur' oversight, and heaven knows, no service is plagued with more 'amateur experts', more ignorant know-alls, more pompously pontificating pundits, and more arrogant bureaucrats ... No public authority would dream of telling doctors how to treat patients nor should they tell teachers how to teach children.

Evidently the teachers were preparing to resist any assault on their own power whether from public authorities or from governors via Taylor. But, equally evident, these assaults were in the making. The interesting point, though, is that they would be mutually exclusive. For if central government were to grab more power still, then there would be little left for the governors to assume. And if Taylor made an irresistible plea for the governors, then central government would have to step back again. The implications were great. Power in central hands would create a tendency towards a more uniform curriculum and possible loss of liberty; dispersal of power would tend towards greater fragmentation.

Notes

1. Shirley Williams, in a lecture delivered at Birkbeck College, December 1977.
2. Tawney, R. H., *Secondary Schools for all* (Allen and Unwin, 1922).
3. Each school has a governing body, sometimes known as a managing body in the case of primary schools.
4. For a review of this evidence, see Nigel Wright, *Progressive Education* (Croom Helm, 1977).
5. One heavyweight analysis – Gray, John, and Satterby, David, 'A Chapter of Errors', in *Educational Research*, November 1976 – said of Bennett's analysis that 'no valid conclusions can be reached on the basis of the published evidence'.
6. Marshall, Sybil, *An Experiment in Education* (Cambridge University Press, 1963).
7. Annual conference, Council of Local Education Authorities (C.L.E.A.), Brighton, July 1977.
8. Opening address at the 11th Annual Plowden Conference, in Lincoln, August 1977.
9. See above pp. 51 and 78.
10. For this and ensuing facts about the primary curriculum the main source is Sheila Browne's C.L.E.A. address. The opinions are my own.
11. Lunn, Joan C. Barker, *Streaming in the Primary School* (N.F.E.R., 1970). See Nigel Wright, on misrepresentations and for wider discussion of research evidence.
12. Newbold, David, *Ability Grouping – the Banbury Enquiry* (N.F.E.R., 1977).
13. Quoted by Devlin, Tim, and Warnock, Mary, in *What Must We Teach?* (Temple Smith, 1977).
14. Schools Council, *Mixed-ability Teaching in Mathematics* (Evans/Methuen Educational, 1977).
15. Reid, Margaret, articles in *The Times Educational Supplement*, 10 June 1977.
16. *Modern Languages in Comprehensive Schools*, H.M.I. series:

'Matters for discussion', No. 3. (H.M.S.O., 1977).

17. *Mathematics, Science and Modern Languages in Maintained Schools in England.* An appraisal of problems in some key subjects by H.M. Inspectorate (D.E.S., 1977).

18. 'Internal Organisation of Schools', in *Aspects of Comprehensive Education,* Papers by H.M. Inspectorate (D.E.S., 1977).

19. *Gifted Children in Middle and Comprehensive Secondary Schools* (H.M.S.O., 1977).

20. Devlin, Tim, and Warnock, Mary, *What Must We Teach?* (Temple Smith, 1977).

21. In this and the following passage on curricular defects I am relying on Sheila Browne's C.L.E.A. speech, Brighton, July 1977, on the H.M.I. paper 'Some Curricular Issues' in *Aspects of Comprehensive Education* (prepared for the York Conference, December 1977), on the Inspectorate's briefing papers for the regional conferences, and on private conversations. (Incidental published sources will be acknowledged in later footnotes.)

22. 'Curricular Differences for Boys and Girls', *Education Survey* 21 (Department of Education and Science, 1975).

23. December 1977.

24. Tenth Report from the Expenditure Committee, Session 1976–7, 'The Attainments of the School Leaver' (H.M.S.O., 1977).

25. 'Curricular Differences for Boys and Girls', *Education Survey* 21 (Department of Education and Science, 1975).

26. Reported in *Education,* 17 December 1976.

27. See below, p. 145 *et seq.*

28. *Modern Languages in Comprehensive Schools* (H.M.S.O., 1977).

29. ibid.

30. Quoted by Sheila Browne, C.L.E.A. lecture, 1977.

31. 25 November 1977.

32. Address to a D.E.S. course on the secondary curriculum and the needs of society, reprinted in an edited version in *The Times Educational Supplement,* 29 October 1976.

33. National Association of Head Teachers, October 1976.

34. In this passage, I have followed with one or two diversions of my own: Ashby, Sir Eric (now Lord), *Technology and the Academics* (Macmillan, 1958), and Montgomery, R. J., *Examinations* (Longmans, 1965).

35. Montgomery, R. J., *Examinations* (Longmans, 1965). The reference here is to the 'Exeter experiment' rather than to the better-known examinations the following year which also followed the same pattern.

36. See Burgess, Tyrrell, and Pratt, John, *Polytechnics: a report* (Pitman, 1974), a work whose warnings have been justified by subsequent developments in most of the polytechnics.

37. Smith, Sir Alex, 'Wisdom Lost in Knowledge', The Bolland Memorial Lecture, Bristol Polytechnic, 23 March 1976.

38. *First Destination of University Graduates*, 1974–5, (H.M.S.O., 1976).

39. *Day Release*, the report of a committee set up by the Minister of Education under the chairmanship of Mr C. Henniker-Heaton, 1964.

40. E.I.T.B. figures, quoted in *Education*, 13 May 1977.

41. *One Europe One Environment*, European Environmental Bureau, Vautierstraat 31, B-1040 Brussels, 1977 (or via the Civic Trust, London).

42. N.U.T. careers conference, October 1977.

43. *Young People and Work*, a report on the feasibility of a new programme of opportunities for the young. (Manpower Services Commission, 1977 – known as the Holland Report).

44. *Education, The Great Debate* (N.U.T. preparatory document, 1977).

45. *Training for the Vital Skills* (Manpower Services Commission, 1977), quoted in *Education, The Great Debate* (N.U.T. preparatory document).

46. *The Sunday Times*, 31 July 1977.

47. Lord Porchester, speaking for industry, made the interesting suggestion at the London regional conference that employers should perhaps be required to engage a specified proportion of young people when recruiting.

48. Reported in *The Times Educational Supplement*, 4 March 1977.

49. Whitehead, A. N., *Science and the Modern World,* (Cambridge, 1927, quoted in Ashby, Sir Eric, *Technology and the Academics* (Macmillan, 1958).

50. The phrase is taken from an outstanding article on school and work by George Walker in *The Times Educational Supplement*, 27 January 1978. It is highly recommended as a starting point for further pursuit of this subject.

51. On all of these questions the best and most thorough review of

evidence is to be found in Nigel Wright's *Progress in Education*. Though Wright clearly has his own political stance – and it is very far removed from that of the Black Paper writers – he is scrupulous in separating fact from opinion.

52. Pedley, Robin, *The Comprehensive School* (Penguin, 2nd ed. 1969).
53. Ross, J. M., *et al.*, *A Critical Appraisal of Comprehensive Education* (National Foundation for Education Research, 1972).
54. Baldwin, R. W., *The Great Comprehensive Gamble* (Helios Press, 1975).
55. *The Times Educational Supplement*, 25 March 1977.
56. Dorothy Davis in *The Times Educational Supplement*, 25 March 1977.
57. Quoted by Shirley Williams, address to the Association of Assistant Mistresses, March 1977. Scores of eleven-year-olds for the whole country in tests by the N.F.E.R. were: 1955, 28.71; 1970, 29.38; 1976, 31.07.
58. *Mathematics, Science and Modern Languages in Maintained Schools,* (D.E.S., 1977).
59. *Modern Languages in Comprehensive Schools,* (H.M.S.O., 1977).
60. These figures were quoted by Shirley Williams in the House of Commons 17 February 1977.
61. Willmott, Alan S., *C.S.E. and G.C.E. Grading Standards: the 1973 Comparability Study* (Schools Council Research Studies/Macmillan Education, 1977).
62. Tenth Report from the Expenditure Committee Session 1976–7, 'The Attainments of the School Leaver' (H.M.S.O., 1977).
63. 26 September 1976.
64. A vision conjured up by Dr Desmond Nuttall, in 'Examinations and Education', a paper presented to the Eugenics Society Symposium on Equalities and Inequalities in Education, September 1974.
65. This was one of the most striking findings of the *Sunday Times* survey referred to above. Though they *said* they attached enormous importance to exam results, leading employers in practice rated qualities which were *not* developed by exams or the work preceding them a good deal more highly than the qualities which were.
66. Entwistle, Noel, and Wilson, John, *Degrees of Excellence* (Hodder and Stoughton, 1977).

67. The mechanisms pushing in this direction were described clearly by Michael Dixon in the *Financial Times*, 18 September 1975.

68. Willmott, A. S., and Nuttall, D. L. *The Reliability of Examinations at 16+* (Macmillan, 1975).

69. Forrest, G. M., *Standards in Subjects at the Ordinary Level of the G.C.E., June 1970* (J.M.B., 1971). Findings broadly confirmed by Nuttall, D., Backhouse, J. K., and Willmott, A. S., in *Comparability of Standards between Subjects*, Schools Council Examinations Bulletin 29 (Evans/Methuen, 1974).

70. *The Whole Curriculum 13 to 16*, Schools Council working paper No. 53.

71. *Pupils in Profile* (Hodder and Stoughton for The Scottish Council for Research in Education, 1977).

72. Taylor, Philip H., Reid, W. A., and Holley, B. J., *The English Sixth Form* (Routledge and Kegan Paul, 1974).

73. Yates, Alfred, director of the National Foundation for Educational Research, 'The Measurement of Productivity in Education', address to the North of England conference, January 1976.

74. *Keeping the School Under Review*: A method of self-assessment for schools devised by the I.L.E.A. Inspectorate (I.L.E.A., 1977).

75. Goldstein, Harvey, and Blinkhorn, Steve, *The Times Educational Supplement*, 23 September 1977.

76. See, for example, Martin Leonard writing in *The Times Educational Supplement*, 17 June 1977.

77. 30 September 1977.

78. Hilsum, S., and Strong, Chris, *The Secondary Teacher's Day* (National Foundation for Educational Research, 1978).

79. Forthcoming survey by Dr N. J. Georgiades of Birkbeck College, London, reported in the *Guardian*, 14 November 1977.

80. *Stress in Schools* (N.A.S./U.W.T., 1976).

81. *Occupational Mortality 1970–72* (H.M.S.O., 1978).

82. 2 September 1977 and 4 October 1974. The key comparisons are made in the 1977 article.

83. Morrison, A., and McIntyre, D., *Teachers and Teaching* (Penguin, 2nd ed., 1973).

84. Morrison, A., and McIntyre, D., *Teachers and Teaching* (Penguin, 2nd ed., 1973).

85. *Schools Council Inquiry 1: Young School Leavers* (H.M.S.O., 1968).
86. Smith, Sir Alex, *This is a Community?* (N.U.T., 1977).
87. September 1977.
88. These are discussed in detail in Wright, Nigel, *Progress in Education* (Croom Helm, 1977).
89. Morrison, A., and McIntyre, D., *Teachers and Teaching* (Penguin, 2nd ed., 1973).
90. Hencke, David, *Colleges in Crisis* (Penguin, 1978). This Book spells out in detail the inconsistencies and obsessive secrecy in government policy towards the colleges. I am indebted to Mr Hencke for an advance view of his manuscript.
91. *Teacher Education and Training* (H.M.S.O., 1972).
92. Devlin, Tim, and Warnock, Mary, *What Must We Teach?* (Temple Smith, 1977).
93. Those who doubt this may care to scrutinize, if they can obtain them, the background papers for the conference, 'Towards a national and local policy for in-service training', held in January 1978 by the Advisory Committee on the Supply and Training of Teachers.
94. 11 March 1977.
95. 'Hansard', House of Commons, Vol. 397, 10 March 1944. Quoted in 'The Taylor Report – A New Partnership for our Schools', (H.M.S.O., 1977).
96. '1945 Model Articles', handily set out in an appendix to the Taylor Report.
97. Sofer, Anne, 'Educational Arguments' in *The Yearbook of Social Policy 1977*, ed. Brown, Muriel, and Baldwin, Sally (Routledge and Kegan Paul, 1978).
98. Quoted in Taylor, paragraph 1.12.
99. See *Educating Our Children*, The Role of Formal Inspection by H.M.I. (D.E.S. preparatory paper for regional conferences, 1977).
100. Her C.L.E.A. speech, see above, p. 112 and note.
101. Each local authority makes its own arrangements over the composition and powers of governing bodies. General statements are therefore over-simple. But the picture drawn above, and in the following paragraph, is based on the account given in Taylor, which draws in turn partly on Baron, George, and Howell, D. A., *The Government and Management of Schools* (Athlone Press, 1974).

102. Taylor, paragraph 2.17.
103. *Parents and Teachers*, Schools Council Research Study Series (Macmillan Education, 1976).
104. Maclure, Stuart, *Professionals, Experts and Laymen*, Bulmershe Lecture 1974 (William Smith (Booksellers) Ltd, 35 London Street, Reading).
105. Taylor, paragraphs 6.7 to 6.11.
106. In *Education Management*, a supplement to *Education*, 8 July 1977.

5. City and village

The Great Debate, with its four official topics for discussion, had a lot in common with the middle reaches of the River Oxus, as described by Matthew Arnold. Like this part of the Oxus, the debate was neither majestic nor flowing right on for the polar star. It was instead divided into separate currents, each obliged to strain 'through beds of sand and matted rushy isles'. The issues raised by the agenda items were all extremely complex. Few, if any, clear solutions seemed to be emerging. In addition, the official prospectus totally omitted two topics of great importance. It seemed, therefore, that they might be ignored in the government's future thinking. One of these was the plight of children of minority ethnic groups, especially those who were black or brown, and living in inner cities. The other was the rapidly accelerating closure of village schools, particularly in the most remote rural areas. It was easy to see how the village schools had been left out of the debate. The neglect of country areas is, after all, a standard part of government procedure when Labour is in office. The omission of the inner cities, however, was quite extraordinary, for a report by the Community Relations Commission[1] in 1975 showed that Labour would not have taken office in October 1974 without the vote of the ethnic minorities. That these groups were now ignored seemed to indicate that Labour's real concern was to reassure the disenchanted denizens of suburb and dormer town, that is to say the silent majority. In the event, both the inner cities and the villages forced themselves on public attention. It proved impossible to keep the question of race and education out of the regional conferences. Black speakers were extremely angry at alleged neglect of their children's needs and in the end won a special section in the government's Green Paper. Village schools caught the public eye as parents' group after parents' group was formed to fight the closures. Each campaign was, of course, strictly local but the sheer number of campaigns began to acquire significance. Observing these developments, I started to follow both issues more systematically.

I should acknowledge, though, before reporting back, that I have a personal as well as a professional interest. Long-standing connections with Herefordshire and what used to be the county of Breconshire gave me some awareness of the rural difficulties and led me in that direction when I began to collect material. The second half of this chapter is concerned with Herefordshire schools and the ways in which their problems are representative of other country districts. My involvement with race and education began in a rather more dramatic way.

In the autumn of 1976 I had the opportunity of visiting New York City as one of a group of a dozen people, each of whom (apart from me) represented some aspect of education in Britain. Standing one morning in the South Bronx, in a wasteland of buildings fired by their inhabitants and looking as if a civil war had ended at about breakfast time, I realized that I would never again be able to look at a city as I had done previously. If this was what discrimination and poverty could do to American Blacks and Puerto Ricans, then discrimination and poverty were among the worst evils in the world, not far short of war in the horrors they produced. Many of us, I suspect, felt the same that morning. Several of the group were already (or are now) in positions where they can try to do something about these problems in Britain. They included Bev Woodroffe, an inspector for community relations with the I.L.E.A., Trevor Carter, now president of the Caribbean Teachers Association, and Peter Newsam, who took over as education officer to the I.L.E.A. within two months of his return. The part of this chapter which deals with London will mention some of the activities of these people and their colleagues.

A second observation from the U.S.A. also underlies the chapter. This is that members of the West Indian community in

New York are regarded as being outstandingly talented. It is no rarity to come across West Indians holding high positions in the professions; almost all have managed to avoid the worst effects and pressures of the ghettos. How could it be, I asked myself, that these people who in New York were so alert and confident, humorous and warm, could occupy the degraded and degrading position allotted to them in British society? Part of the answer might well be selective emigration of the most able to New York, but even that, one felt, could not account for the whole of the difference. What was Britain doing to waste the potential of these people?

The broad facts relating to Britain's coloured citizens are so well known that they need only the briefest reference here. The main communities are of West Indian or Asian background. At the time of the 1971 census they numbered about 1,500,000. The number is rather more today, though still short of two million. Almost half of them were born in Britain and that proportion is increasing rapidly because of tighter and tighter limitations on coloured immigration. Most of them live in the poorest areas of the inner cities. They are far more likely than indigenous Britons to suffer from poverty, bad housing and unemployment. Eighteen per cent of all West Indian babies in Britain, for example, are born into what is termed 'multiple deprivation'. The figure for indigenous Britons is 6 per cent. They are heavily and persistently discriminated against. The 1976 Race Relations Act was meant to put an end to this but it still remains the case that a black youngster has to attend four times as many interviews as a young white of similar qualifications before he is likely to find a job.[2] Racialist attitudes are uncovered by every survey of the subject and extreme right-wing political groups have found it easy to stir up ill-feeling. Many black people living here have also been alarmed by talk of compulsory repatriation.

In terms of education the problems are possibly less familiar. The most comprehensive brief summary of them – on which I shall largely rely in the following paragraphs – is to be found in an inaugural lecture delivered at Goldsmith's College in March

1978[3] by Professor Alan Little. The wide-ranging references
and careful footnoting of this lecture will also provide the
reader with an easy way into the literature on the subject.

Most of the points that need to be made spring in a fairly
obvious way from the general situation of the West Indian and
Asian communities. First is the fact that black children are
physically concentrated in just a few cities. In 1972, the D.E.S.
was still keeping statistics of what it called 'immigrants' (the
definition was very rough-and-ready). According to these, there
were two education authority areas where more than 25 per
cent of pupils were classed as immigrant; five local authorities
had between 20 and 25 per cent and another six between 15 and
20 per cent. Today, in Bradford, Birmingham, Leicester, Wol-
verhampton and the G.L.C. area, one fifth or more of current
school entrants are the children of women from the New Commonwealth and Pakistan. 'In areas like these', said Professor
Little in his lecture, the black children are not a small proportion of the school population but a sizeable element and the
issue of their progress in school is a major one facing the school
and the local authority.' Even so, very few schools are made up
almost entirely of black children as happens so often in America. The majority will attend schools where they are themselves in a minority or, at most, level pegging with white
children.

The children suffer the social disadvantages of the adults in
particularly acute form. This is because the schools themselves
become centres of disadvantage by virtue of the high proportion of disadvantaged children congregated in them. This
point was made most forcefully by Professor Raymond Giles
when he observed in his study of West Indians in London that,
so far as teachers were concerned, 'a multi-racial school' was
merely a euphemism for a school with 'a racial and cultural mix
of pupils from needy backgrounds.'[4] Black pupils in these
schools are often the victims of racial discrimination by their
classmates.[5] The Chairman of Manchester Education Committee
has written: 'Many of these children inevitably bear the scars
of social stress. Many are language deprived, under achieving,

display anti-social behaviour.'[6] The combination of social disadvantage, poor performance in school and discrimination on grounds of colour means a difference in the *quality* of misfortune as well as its quantity. One consequence is the alienation of young black people about which there have been so many warnings. All of these problems afflict the West Indian community even more seriously than they do the Asian. One reason sometimes advanced is that most Asian settlers have a strong culture and value system of their own. But West Indian culture derives extensively from British. Feeling themselves rejected by the British people, West Indians therefore have no 'fall back' position. I am not myself entirely convinced by this explanation even though it has been put forward by a number of serious researchers. But whatever the cause, the situation is extremely grave for the West Indian community, slightly less so for the Asian.

In education, however, there is little by way of government policy designed to set things right. As the Select Committee on Race Relations and Immigration said in 1972–3, in speaking of educational policies: 'One conclusion which stands out above all others is that we have failed to grasp and are still failing to grasp the scale of what we have taken on.' Successive governments have confined themselves mainly to offering advice, based on the proposition that speedy assimilation is the best hope. The D.E.S. circular 7/65, issued in June 1965, advised that no school should have more than one third immigrant children. Fortunately, perhaps, in the light of American experience with bussing, the policy of dispersal never took hold. Rather more helpful advice has been published during the 1970s. But none of it amounts to any kind of strategy. As far as money is concerned, there are two sources. Local authorities can apply to the government for 75 per cent of the wages of staff hired specifically because of the presence in their area of large numbers of 'immigrants from the Commonwealth whose language and customs differ from those of the community'. But payments are retrospective, somewhat inflexible and depend on the sharpness and goodwill of the local authority in making the application in the first place. Naturally, the take-up has been uneven. A working party of chief education officers convened by the Community Relations Commission[7] complained that in its use of this so-called Section 11 money[8] the government had failed to associate itself with local authorities 'to achieve the identification of needs, desirable levels of provision and objectives'. In other words, there was no policy. The other source of money is the Urban Programme, recently much augmented. This is based quite clearly and specifically on the philosophy of providing special help to everybody suffering from educational disadvantage, rather than on making special provision for the black community. This has the great political advantage of being unlikely to provoke a white backlash. But it goes only the smallest way towards meeting the special and different problems of black people. The Runnymede Trust has estimated that by the mid-1970s only 5 per cent of urban aid money went specifically to black projects. This is the difficulty with 'colourblind' provision.

Some people, among them Professor Little, believe that the only answer is massive activity by central government, working closely with local authorities and providing a special fund for community schools in areas where black people are concentrated. But in a political climate in which specific grants for education have been ruled out, a central fund seems most improbable. That being so, the local authorities remain, as they always have been, the real centres of policy-making in race and education. During 1977 I spent some time in Liverpool and Birmingham trying to find out what was happening there. Rather to my surprise, both authorities were behaving a good deal more actively than one might have assumed from the vacuum in central policy.

Liverpool is particularly interesting because it has had a black population for more than 100 years. In 1973 the city was harshly criticized by the parliamentary Select Committee on Race Relations because it did not do enough for its black youngsters. The committee felt that if matters were as bad as they seemed on Merseyside after 100 years then omens were extremely poor for other cities. In response to the criticism, Liverpool is now trying to 'make itself over'. The difficulties are immense; the steps are uncertain and small in relation to the difficulties; but the direction of the steps may turn out to be significant.

Nawab Khan sits in a first floor office in an old school building. Its windows look out on to empty spaces lightly strewn with litter. Beyond are the dilapidated terraces of Liverpool 8. The university and two cathedrals lie among them like stranded whales. Mr Khan's job is to push an idea which is relatively new in Britain – namely that people have a right to be British in their own way, and that if they are black they should be proud of it, respecting their own culture and entitled to respect from the rest of us. This is cultural pluralism. It is an ideal quite different from the conventional assumption that if the melting pot boils long enough we will all come out roughly the same. By Liverpool's new theory, black people have a right both to belong and to be different.

'When I began this job in January 1976 we had no blueprint, no guidelines,' said Mr Khan. 'But we have two major aims which make our work relevant to all the city's schools. These are respect for oneself – self-image, that is to say – and respect for other people.' Too often, deep down inside, black children hold themselves in low esteem. They must be given back their dignity in their own eyes, he says, and this is unlikely to happen unless they are also treated with dignity by others.

Much of the theory which Mr Khan propounds was endorsed by a local authority working party which created, among a number of other initiatives, the job Mr Khan holds today as the city's first teacher-adviser in multi-ethnic education. The committee also drew up a set of background papers which spelled out the reasons for tackling the problems vigorously. One of them described how black children *below the age of five* might pick up from society at large a notion of themselves as dirty, lazy and noisy, how this self-image was reinforced at school, leading often to obsessive concern, self-hate and aggression by a child towards his own racial group. This might be followed by withdrawal or clowning and finally by reliance on the in-group, with aggression and violence directed at those outside. Meanwhile, the teacher's original stereotype of black pupils would receive daily confirmation.

To the working party it appeared vital to put these facts to the teachers, the more so since they were unlikely to absorb them of their own volition. 'Demand is unlikely to arise spontaneously', said one of the papers, 'as there has been relatively little national publicity about multi-racial education, some of which has even been counter-productive, and teachers, especially those in non-multiracial schools, do not perceive it to be relevant to the situation in which they find themselves.' This 'what, me?' attitude is very prevalent among teachers[9] and remains the biggest obstacle to any genuine cultural pluralism. There is also a strong tendency among teachers, based on the highest principles, to ignore the ethnic origins of their children. They feel that to take race into account is itself an act of racism. Unfortunately, they may, by the same token, ignore the special nature of black children's problems and fail to take advantage of the cultural diversity of the classroom.

In Liverpool's case, an opportunity at least to put across the basic information about race was provided by the city's induction scheme for new teachers. Under this scheme all recruits to the teaching force attend regular courses. In these the main facts of discrimination and disadvantage are now presented. Practical suggestions for teaching include, in infant and junior school, the use of pictures reflecting a multi-racial society; in junior school, the inclusion of material on minority groups in reading and discussion; and for secondary pupils, visits by members of varying ethnic groups, improvised drama and role playing, evaluation of newspapers and magazines. Interestingly, Black Studies are not proposed, the feeling being that it is the whole curriculum which should be permeated with multi-cultural assumptions. And the point is hammered home relentlessly that 'the main factor is the teacher's own outlook'. In another campaign, some of the most colonial-minded history and geography books have been weeded out of school libraries.

But the business of changing attitudes is hard work. 'If we could make people realize the relevance of multi-racial education within two or three years, then we will have done something,' says Mr Khan.

In Birmingham there is a substantial West Indian community, and an even larger concentration of Asians. Most of them live in the city's dingy inner ring which is spiritually at a far remove from the leafy suburbs of the periphery. In Birmingham, as in Liverpool, the local authority is trying to infuse into the teaching force a sympathetic understanding and the kind of practical skills that are needed to cope. On one of my two visits to the city during the preparation of this book I was in the company of a party of return visitors from New York City. We saw a host of enterprising projects. Most involved attempts to bring the community into the schools and, at primary school level, to create a genuinely multi-racial setting. This was not so evident in the secondary schools.

To some of the American visitors with their knowledge of how far a city can degenerate, much of what we saw seemed, on the whole, small beer. One middle-school principal commented darkly that there was a 'terrible problem'. 'You have this problem,' he said, 'because you have not brought the situation of the ethnic minorities right up into your consciousness. Head after head, teacher after teacher, has not realized the extent of this problem.' To me it seemed that a real beginning had been made. This impression was particularly strong in everything to do with the teaching of the English language.

Lack of English, as most readers will know, is the main educational problem of the Asian community in Britain. In school, the children are well-motivated and industrious and once they are fluent in English they perform about as well as indigenous children. But some dependent children are still arriving. Most of these speak only Asian languages. Many of those born here have been brought up in households where no English is known. Many of the mothers cannot manage a simple sentence in English and so remain cut off from the social services, even from medical attention.

To those working in the field the plight of the 'born here' child seems worse than that of the child 'brought over'. Bob Chapman, Birmingham's inspector for multi-racial education and English as a second language, explains that the 'brought-over' child is in contact with many people throughout his developing years, particularly the old. 'I have photos I've taken in India of babies sitting on a grandmother's knee, the little hand following the spinning wheel. The grandmothers talk all the time. There's tremendous concept formation. Just think of weaving. This gives them colour, size, sorting, thick or thin, too much, too little, too short, too long. They live in a sharing community and have a good number of fully formed concepts in their own language.' The non-English speaking child born in this country will have had few or none of these advantages. His mother will probably have been isolated by housing and climate and, if she is a Muslim, will perhaps be in semi-Purdah. The result is that the children may be complete strangers, looking out 'like goldfish from a bowl'. 'They come to school not ready for it, with little language and few concepts. These children need tremendous language help, far more than the brought-over child.'

To meet the pressing needs both of the children born here and of those brought over, Birmingham had by 1977 a team of ninety-two peripatetic English language teachers. Most of these fan out each day from the city's Language Centre at Hockley to work with over 4,600 children in seventy-eight primary schools. They take the children in special withdrawal groups for several hours a week, doing their best to give them the rudiments of English. But for much of the time the children stay in their regular classes, on the theory that almost all the activities of a well-ordered primary classroom tend towards the development of language.

There are many courses for teachers, both in their own schools and in the Language Centre. These stress not just the importance of language but also the great cultural richness available to any multi-racial school which cares to take advantage of it. They also put over basic information, such as that children may become fractious when they have not eaten between sunrise and sunset during the whole of the lunar month of Ramadan. The Centre has a wide variety of multi-cultural materials for teachers to use, ranging from musical instruments to works of art. It is becoming quite a popular place. Eric Payne, a West Indian teacher on the staff there, says, 'Hardly a day goes by that the phone doesn't ring saying "We have so many non-English speakers. Could somebody please come in?" '

For secondary-age children who speak no English there are three full-time reception centres where, for up to a year, they receive special language teaching in groups of just sixteen. They also do all the main school subjects in simplified form so that they will have the necessary vocabulary when they are finally placed in ordinary schools. They are even given lessons in football.

'They are being educated now, not minded,' says Val Hasan, head of the Main Street Centre in Sparkhill. 'It's a far cry from the days when they were sent off into a corner with a magazine or put in a remedial group.' Many who started in the centres have now successfully completed their secondary education, with a satisfying proportion moving on to university or higher education. In the top group, where a written exercise was in progress at the time of my visit, the concentration was intense, the English of those with whom I spoke was clear and generally competent. 'It's a wonderful thing for our people, having these centres,' said K. M. Malik, the teacher.

Most of the cities settled by Asians, and not forgetting Liverpool with its Chinese community, have evolved some kind of language policy, though in many cases less impressive than that of Birmingham. Bradford and Ealing deserve a special word of praise. There is also a problem, now increasingly appreciated, with the language patterns of West Indian children. Creole, patois or even such variants as London Jamaican, all with their own grammatical structure, may interfere with the acquisition of orthodox English. Because the children are basically English speaking, it is easy for teachers to interpret these difficulties as a

sign of stupidity. Today, in cities such as London and Birmingham it is now, more and more often, realized that special
and more subtle help is needed.

All these developments in language teaching may take place
perfectly consistently within an integrationist framework. One
other possibility – that of teaching the child the ordinary school
subjects in his own home language or 'mother-tongue' – is
nowadays more and more discussed. 'It will come,' says Bob
Chapman of Birmingham, 'There's no doubt about it.'

The theory is that a child who is weak in concepts will be able
to build them better in his own language. The maintenance of
the mother tongue may also help heal a growing gap in many
families where the children, having learnt English, move
away from their parents into a private world. Most important
of all, perhaps, is the improvement that may occur in the child's
self-image. 'They need pride in their own language and culture,'
says Chapman, 'and to see society giving them positive recognition. If *we* were going to China would we be prepared to
submerge our own language? To feel comfortable in society
makes one a better citizen. Two years ago there was a conference on this in Leicester. Not many people were convinced.
Today there's a strong groundswell for mother-tongue teaching.
It's coming from individual families who a few years ago were
determined to learn English, and just English, as soon as possible.'

There are two possible strategies with mother-tongue teaching. One is to use the mother-tongue only until children are
strong enough in English to transfer into that language for their
basic studies. Aternatively, the mother tongue might be used
throughout school life. The implications of these approaches
obviously differ. But either would involve a high degree of cultural pluralism. Integrationists are bitterly critical of the idea
because they say it is divisive. American evidence tends to
confirm this. On the other hand, it can be argued, as it is in
America, that there is no equality of opportunity for children
obliged to learn everything in a language foreign to them. What
they need is their own language *and* the language of the country

where they are living. Parents in many communities already support private schools to keep the children's mother tongue alive. Many believe it is a matter in which state education has a responsibility; and this principle is built into an E.E.C. directive on the teaching of migrant workers' children which Britain signed in 1977. Because of this, and because more and more people are thinking like Bob Chapman, we are going to hear a lot about this issue in the future.[10]

In London, the problems are those of scale and diversity, though within that diversity the difficulties of West Indian children are the greatest. The number of foreign communities in the city is enormous – Irish, Russians, Poles, Bengalis in Spitalfields, Chinese in Soho, rural Moroccans now settling in north Kensington. In one primary school in the Portobello Road area more than twenty languages are represented. The problem of scale may be gathered from the fact that Inner London has 25 per cent of the West Indian population of the whole country. The pattern of concentration is also particularly striking in Inner London. For while some boroughs remain mostly white (Greenwich is an example), others have become home to many black people. In 1975, 26 per cent or more of live births in Hackney, Islington, Lambeth, Tower Hamlets and Wandsworth, were to mothers born in the New Commonwealth or Pakistan.

West Indian children in these and other areas are doing very badly in school. Only half of the expected number figure in the top ability band at time of transfer to secondary school. At the same point, West Indian children are on average a year behind the national norm in reading. They are doing significantly worse even than other disadvantaged sections of the community.[11] A complex of factors (identified by Professor Michael Rutter, in his consistently illuminating research[12]) causes them to be rated lower than expected on I.Q. tests. This has the consequence, nationwide, that many have ended up wrongly placed at schools for educationally subnormal children, a matter which causes dismay and anger among West Indian parents. Little of this poor performance seems to be necessary. West Indians as a whole can do extremely well when conditions are favourable. New York proves the point. Even in Britain, when child and the right teacher come together at the right time, the results of individuals often improve sharply, demonstrating that previous low performance was due to something other than stupidity. Many individuals, though not enough to change the statistical picture, do consistently well despite their social handicaps.

Educationally the basic problems of Inner London are those of language for non-English speakers, the underperformance of West Indian children, and the need to encourage a multi-cultural approach throughout a school system that is profoundly and permanently multi-cultural. Attempts to deal with language follow roughly the same lines as in Birmingham; and in the paragraphs which follow I shall therefore concentrate on multi-culturalism and the prospects of West Indian children. But before we turn to these, it is essential to look at a problem Inner London shares with almost every other education authority. That is the declining school population. It is the single most important factor in educational planning in the cities today; and the decline could lead with equal ease either to disaster or to great advantage.

The critical question is the future of the teachers. In Inner London it is expected that the primary school population will drop from its 1976 total of 180,000 to 118,000 in 1986. In 1976 the teacher–pupil ratio was 1:20 and there were 9000 teachers. If the authority could somehow raise the money to keep them all, the ratio in 1986 would drop to 1:13. That would be to the enormous advantage of the schools, and it is obviously in the interests of the I.L.E.A. to have as many teachers as it can. Up to the spring of 1978, the authority had in fact managed to retain its full, original complement and was using many of the newly surplus teachers to tackle multi-ethnic problems. But it was clear that the I.L.E.A. would be unable to hold the situation for ever. Keeping all the teachers would mean vastly increased expenditure on each child, financed by rates drawn from a dwindling tax base. If, to take the other extreme, teaching jobs were reduced *pro rata* so that the ration remained at

1:20, there would be 3100 fewer primary teachers in 1986. This seems no more likely to come about than the alternative ratio of 1:13. In practice, ratios will probably improve somewhat and the number of teaching posts will simultaneously decline. But the decline will be steep and it is here that the real difficulties lie.

From the authority's point of view, and more important, perhaps, from the children's point of view, a decline in numbers opens up the possibility of getting rid of the worst teachers. In a system the size of the I.L.E.A. there are inevitably several hundred who are not very good. If these are not identified, not only will an opportunity be lost, but the system will actually get worse. This is because the most able and far-sighted are generally the first to spot trouble and make other arrangements. The possibility therefore arises of a concentration of bad teachers. Another problem is that unless some of the older teachers choose to leave, it will be impossible, for perhaps a decade, to hire any younger teachers at all. A gap like this would throw the teaching force right out of balance, with potentially deadening consequences. Therefore, if it is to improve its service rather than see it spoiled, the I.L.E.A. has to get rid of bad teachers, starting now. The same applies to almost every big city in Britain. This is a problem which has been exercising the government. The difficulty is that any kind of voluntary severance which was financially attractive to bad teachers would be just as attractive to the good ones. The only alternative is involuntary severance. Yet how could this be done without creating such paranoia and strife that the system would in any case be destroyed? And how could any administrator contemplate the dismissal of a teacher who had given his working life, however inefficiently, to the service of children?

Unfortunately, the question of what to do about falling rolls is already upon us in the primary schools. In five or six years' time it will be working its way into the secondary schools. The potential disruption it may cause is quite unquantifiable. All that is certain is that something, somewhere, will have to give, not only in Inner London but throughout the country. We are probably about to witness a systemic change which may be more important in its consequences, for better or for worse, than comprehensive reorganization itself.

It is against this threatening cloudscape that the I.L.E.A. is trying to do something which central government has not ventured to attempt. That is to introduce a city-wide policy of positive help for all ethnic minorities – and to do so within a context of cultural pluralism.

Nobody who stood with Peter Newsam in the South Bronx will be much surprised that Inner London's new policy has come into being within a year of his taking over as education officer at the I.L.E.A. Much was, of course, already going on, with many projects developing quite strongly and the appointment of specialist I.L.E.A. inspectors. But the situation in the schools was extremely poor, above all from a West Indian point of view. Professor Giles[13] described the difficulties of teachers as he saw them in 1976:

Many of the teachers in the schools I visited, in disadvantaged areas of London, had had no previous contact with culturally different children. There was no policy to guide them. They had had no special preparation or training, and most of them admitted that their own personal background and experience had been woefully limited in terms of exposure to culturally diverse people or environments. On coming to these schools, they did not know how to comprehend or assess sophisticated notions of cultural pluralism, or how to consider cultural pluralism's implication in the revision of curriculum.

The new policy was designed to meet the very extensive problems both in the teaching force and among the ethnic-minority groups. One of its most important aspects was that it was adopted with bi-partisan support. This meant that it was likely to continue whether Labour or Conservatives were in power in the I.L.E.A.

There were six main elements in the policy. The first was a strong declaration that the I.L.E.A. was committed to providing the best possible opportunities for all its children. Since it was the ethnic minorities who were in such trouble, this meant positive discrimination, the second plank in the policy. Nothing would be taken away from other children; but more attention and resources than at present would be concentrated on minorities. The third plank, a vital one, was far deeper consultation with the minority groups themselves. (This began late in 1977 when even such traditionally non-participant communities as the Chinese began to come forward with their ideas.) The fourth was the collection of statistics on the ethnic origins of staff and students 'where these statistics have a specifically educational purpose'. This was extremely controversial. The D.E.S. had abandoned its statistics on 'immigrants' in 1974, partly because of difficulties of definition. The teachers regarded the collection of statistics as racialist. So did many black groups. Since then it has become apparent that it is extremely hard to deal with any of the problems of race in the absence of proper knowledge. Many black groups have changed their minds. (Some have not, because of apprehension about how statistics might be used.) The teacher unions have substantially softened their line and the D.E.S. is in active consultations over starting up again. In this atmosphere the I.L.E.A. took the initiative and began to negotiate with London teachers on the collection of facts and figures.

The other main elements in the policy are the strengthening of the inspectorate and administration, and backing for specific projects to bring into the classroom the richness of a diverse society. A problem which has not yet been solved anywhere in Britain is also getting serious thought. This is how to find enough black teachers. The cultural contribution of Asians and West Indians is badly needed in the classroom. Their presence would demonstrate that positions of responsibility are open to all races.

As I write, the new policy remains a matter of aspiration. The problems are vast and the I.L.E.A. lacks power of direction over individual schools. It is not seeking these powers but it has to find a way of making policy stick. Otherwise it will be mostly a matter of words. And that, it seems, will be nothing like good enough. Stephen Aiello, president of New York City's Board of Education in 1977 and the man responsible for running the system, was one of the New York group who visited Birmingham and later London. On the day he left he gave me his opinion. It went like this: 'From what we've seen here, which is very limited, there seems at least some basis for comparison between where London and Birmingham are right now over race relations in schools, and where we were fifteen years ago. If attitudes anywhere remain that there's nothing we want to do about this, or that the problem is minor and will somehow evaporate into the air, then I'm afraid British society faces the same kind of turmoil and tumult that American society faced, and continues to face.'

Herefordshire is somewhat different from the inner cities. It offers a landscape where nine tenths of every prospect pleases. The red and white cattle, the black and white villages, the serpentine rivers, moorland and apple orchards all combine to suggest a land at peace. That things are not so simple was quickly apparent when I set out in the summer of 1977 on a series of school visits in the former county (now part of the conglomerate of Hereford and Worcester). On most of these visits I was fortunate in having the company and comments of Pam Sherlock, whose work as an Open University tutor in the teaching of reading has given her an extensive knowledge of local schools. It took very little time to establish a fact already well known to Mrs Sherlock – namely that children in remote rural areas may suffer from many of the same troubles as inner-city children. As in the city, and leaving aside the question of race, the worst of these spring from poverty and lack of human contact.

In school after school we were told that children from isolated farms and cottages could speak scarcely more than a few words when they first arrived in class. 'I've got ten little ones this year,' said one infant teacher in the south of Herefordshire. 'Six of them didn't know colours and couldn't count at all. They didn't know games like ring-a-ring-a-roses or Farmers in the Dell. They didn't know stories or nursery rhymes.' In a modest experiment in the north we circulated among a class of first-year infants picking out those who seemed to have the greatest difficulty in putting their thoughts into words. Without exception, we found that these children came from remote addresses. Their parents, we gathered from the teachers, were often hard-pressed economically and extremely busy trying to make ends meet. Probably the children were spoken to as little as children in high-rise flats in Liverpool or Glasgow. Perhaps there were no other children nearby, and, if there were, of the wrong age for them to become friends or playmates. And pre-school play groups, though on the increase, might well be miles away from homes which lacked transport.

'This means that country children lag behind in conversation,' said Tegwyn Griffiths, then head of the primary school in Weobley, a stunningly beautiful Elizabethan village. 'It makes it much harder for them when it comes to writing things down.' 'What you notice first is that the children don't talk very much,' says David Barrah, head of Shobdon primary, another village school. 'When they are at home they are busy fishing or playing down by the stream. Their homes are very, very scattered. The mums will tell you that the kids are dying to get back to school after the holidays so that they can see their friends. Socializing is one of the main functions of country schools. What the children need is masses and masses of talk.'

These unsystematic impressions were confirmed at every turn by those who had approached the question quantitatively. Dennis O'Donnell is now an administrator in the county's education service. In the early 1970s, as head of Queen Elizabeth High School in Bromyard, he discovered that while fifteen-year-olds from his highly rural catchment area performed at about national average in non-verbal reasoning tests (mainly involving mathematical and spatial brain-teasers), the same pupils were significantly below average at tests involving verbal skills. An educational psychologist in the county told me that acute language problems of a non-neurological kind cropped up continuously. Though one would expect to meet only about one case in 10,000 children, she herself picked out each year from the 200 sent to her some twenty in this category – 'statistically, a staggering number, totally disproportionate'.

'And as one would expect, language difficulties are often paralleled by other troubles. Roland Summers is headmaster of Whitecross, a Hereford City comprehensive which also draws from the surrounding countryside. His previous job had been in St Helens near Liverpool. Arriving in Herefordshire, he anticipated a vast difference in terms of the personal welfare of his pupils. 'But there isn't,' he said. 'There are just as many broken homes, just as much distress. The problems are harder to see in rural surroundings, that's all.'

Educational psychologists, who get a concentrated view of all problems, again confirmed this impression. We were told of a family who had to live for three weeks in a chicken hutch for lack of other shelter, of another family living in a house stinking of urine and with part of the wall and roof caved in, of a family where the father had had a heart attack through overwork, the mother had artheriosclerosis and all the water had to be fetched from the brook. These, of course, were the extremes, but even so the picture seemed closer to the poverty described a hundred years ago in Kilvert's diary than to what one might anticipate today.

But does this mean, as one might reasonably expect, that country schools are dreadful? The answer, unequivocally, is no. Often, they seem to be doing a quite outstanding job. In Shobdon, Garway, Weobley and St Weonards, in Hereford, Peterchurch and Michaelchurch in Escley I visited schools that were in sound working order and in many cases having some success in helping pupils escape from isolation into sociability.

Take, for example, Michaelchurch Escley, a hamlet high-up under the long eastern ridge of the Black Mountains. Its physical isolation is paralleled by that of the village school, which is surrounded on all sides by farmland.

It is not a big school. In the summer of 1977 it had eleven infants, aged from four to six, and twenty-one juniors aged from seven to eleven, a total of thirty-two children on the school roll. It is not tremendously progressive either. The infants do reading, writing and arithmetic all morning and have an element of choice only in the afternoon. 'Children like to be told,' says Margaret Price, the infant teacher. 'These educationalists can say what they want about children going to school and pleasing themselves. They get into an absolute fog.'

In the juniors, Jeff Parker, grey-haired and wearing a tie with badgers' heads on it, has single-handedly to meet the needs of every pupil, despite differences in age and ability. There is always a little knot of children round his desk offering exercise books for correction or bringing him questions they cannot answer for themselves. Waving them cheerfully away, he breaks off to observe that teachers in rural areas have a duty to know the language of the country. When they ask a child to identify an animal, says Mr Parker, and he replies not 'cow' but 'Hereford Friesian cross heifer', they have to understand exactly what he means. Today, he thinks, it may even be up to the teachers to preserve the strength and singularity of rural culture. In common with many Herefordshire teachers he believes that television is ironing these out and reckons it his special task to remind the children – occasionally – of such usages as 'quist' for woodpigeon and 'oontitump' for molehill. ('Glatting a hedge', I am glad to say, is still in frequent use on the surrounding farms and deep into Breconshire as well. 'Glatting' means patching up the holes.)

One difficulty though, as Mr Parker points out, is that most of the teacher training colleges which once specialized in rural education are currently being closed. 'Young teachers today come from the conurbations, they are trained in the conurbations and they go back to the conurbations to work.'

As we talk I become aware that the isolation of the school, and the lack of fellow-teachers to observe what goes on in the two classrooms, mean that the opportunities for unadventurous or even lazy teaching are immense. But half an hour in the school makes it plain that Michaelchurch Escley is not like that at all. For a start, most of the older juniors can read, write and calculate to a standard that only the brighter children would achieve in some more troubled inner-city schools. The children's pictures make it plain that fantasy has not been thrown out of the window in order to achieve this result. One picture shows, for instance, a group of ghouls dancing in a graveyard in the most morbid manner, another a white house on the shores of a lake in an infinite wilderness. The children themselves are a little shy, certainly, but friendly to a visitor and inescapably swept up in the cooperative atmosphere of the school.

'You, you and you, fetch us the ladder,' says headmaster Parker, naming three boys. 'Now then, Susan, what's the problem here?' The three boys go off with pleasure to get a ladder, visibly restraining the urge to run through the classroom. (It is needed for a photographer accompanying me on this, my second visit.)

I am puzzled by the sunniness of the atmosphere, the ease of relationships in a classroom where discipline is clearly a main requirement. But then an explanation occurs. In this tiny school, with sheep browsing outside the window and nothing else but clouds in visible movement, children and teachers are on the same side. They make a common front. They are, if this does not sound too much like optimism in a pessimistic era, a family in the classroom.

A good deal of the same atmosphere obtains at the comprehensive school just down the road at Peterchurch. With 180 pupils, this is one of the smallest in the country, taking children from eleven to sixteen. Those who want to continue with their studies go on to the sixth-form college in Hereford. The college is a large institution, necessarily and properly wide in outlook. But the school at Peterchurch makes it its business to meet the needs of its own area as precisely as it can and reckons its small size is an important means to that end. Ronald Collett, the headmaster, says: 'After fifteen years here, I'm absolutely opposed to the principle of the large comprehensive. In a truly rural area many parents who are close to the land do not really see the value of the kind of education offered to their children. Many of the children are very reserved because of the isolation. Children like this require a good deal of attention in their early years of secondary school. But once they get the bit between their teeth they are as fully able as their counterparts in urban areas to take advantage of education. We can give the help they need in a small school.' (One of the most important arguments advanced in favour of small schools is the easy and often pleasant access they afford to parents.)

The atmosphere in the classrooms at Peterchurch is pleasant, while fairly strict. There is a school garden which is the scene of much study of biological principle. But though the school takes the Associated Examining Board's rural biology syllabus at 'O' level, there isn't an overwhelming concentration on rural matters. This is because only a minority of children finally take jobs on farms.

The staff is extremely stable, almost too stable, some might say, with just three changes of full-timers in fifteen and a half years. (Mr Collett himself retired soon after my visit.) And though one of the great drawbacks of small secondary schools is said to be the difficulty of maintaining a full and varied curriculum, twenty-one subjects are offered at 'O' level and the same at C.S.E. Mrs Sherlock and I scrutinize the exam results and find them outstanding on any computation – so much so that one might wonder if this aspect of school was over-emphasized.

Summarizing our visits, Mrs Sherlock says – and I agree: 'Country children take a long time to reach a high standard. But they are perfectly capable of it. They do best when they start in small and quiet schools.'

This makes it almost tragic that both Michaelchurch Escley and Peterchurch – two schools appearing to offer precisely the service best suited to their clients – are under threat of imminent closure. Michaelchurch Escley's fate is already decided. The children will have to go four miles away to Longtown, where expensive adaptation to the buildings is now in progress. This will more than double the journey for some of them.

Peterchurch has already fought off three attempts at closure, getting its friends to battle for it right up to county council level. But its future is to be reviewed again in 1981, and the children are likely at some point to be diverted to Kingstone, six miles away. Some Peterchurch pupils on the far side of the catchment area from Kingstone already travel one and a half hours to reach the school.

These two schools are among thousands facing closure in rural areas in England and Wales. *Where*, the magazine of the Advisory Centre for Education, puts the total of threatened primaries at 7000.[14] The number of secondary schools in danger is unknown. It is a serious matter not just for children but for all the people living in rural communities. For the village schools, it seems, provide a focus for a village's identity. Residents fear that once the children are educated elsewhere they will abandon the village spiritually. Parents resent the loss of self-determinism in education. And these feelings run extraordinarily deep, as was revealed when Hereford and Worcester county council carried out a survey in the village of Moccas in 1976. The school was closed in 1948. Here are some of the comments: 'There is a tremendous impact on village life when the school goes – it loses its identity'; 'It makes a big difference, the village falls apart'; 'A village without a school loses its cohesion'; 'When the village school closes, people lose interest in the village'. Those who answered the survey were unhappy about their children's journey to the substitute school – several miles each way – and felt that they were outsiders there when they arrived.

Alan Beith, Liberal M.P. for Berwick-upon-Tweed, drew many of these themes together in a powerful speech in the House of Commons in 1977. One of the points he made was this:

Young families look around for council houses in the towns because they know there is no school for their children. The absence of a school tends to be used by the planning authorities as an argument against any attempt to maintain other community services. They begin to say, 'This is no longer a viable community. It has no school, so there is no logic in maintaining public transport to it. We must treat it as a village that will die a natural death.'

Unfortunately, and even though it has the ring of truth, the community case rests on assertion rather than firm knowledge; there is a considerable dearth of information about what does in fact occur in the wake of a closure. Hereford and Worcester council is currently trying to find out, by keeping tabs on three villages where schools were closed in 1977. The results are likely to have national significance. Nevertheless it is clear that the emotional response alone is something to be reckoned with. Campaigning groups have sprung up around village schools from Cumbria to Cornwall and every announcement of a closure is likely to produce a fresh one. Despite these difficulties, the local authorities persist. Why are they doing it?

Usually, and regardless of the satisfaction expressed by parents, the local authorities claim they are closing the schools so as to offer better education to the children. The most impressive argument for this is that the society of the small school is too constricting, that there may be too little social interaction. Specialist facilities may also be lacking, particularly in music and sport. Village schools may be in general a little backward. Here, for example is the chief education officer of Cambridgeshire, David Spreadbury, as quoted in *Where*, August 1976:

> The danger of vegetating in a backwater is almost inevitable. It is hard for a teacher to provide the opportunities for stimulus and change. In the urban school, problems press in from all sides; but in the village, life is remote, irresponsible, problem-free. Travel is difficult, village children can remain educationally and socially stranded, with few facilities to compensate and no competition to spur them on.

Even Mr Parker of Michaelchurch Escley goes part of the way with this. 'You look at these kiddies,' he says. 'There's only one stimulus from the environment – agriculture and nature studies. But the town child is bombarded with numbers and reading material – "Halt, give way, Steel's garage, prices slashed, tuppence off". All we ever see is "SLOW, MUD".'

Then there is the problem of bad teachers, often put forward in the abstract as part of the reason for closures. In a one-room school a child may be with a single teacher for four years. This means that an inefficient, lazy, stupid or insensitive adult can do incalculably more damage to the individual child. The problem of bad heads can also be acute. Some ambitious teachers try to further their career by getting a village headship at an early age,

even when they have no particular bent for rural education.
Sometimes they can get stuck there for the rest of their working
lives, themselves embittered and poisoning the lives of gener-
ations of children. Worst of all are the occasions when a whole
village falls out with its head-teacher and finds him – usually
him, not her, in country districts – not just immovable but irre-
movable as well.

These are interesting arguments, even though none of them
seems remotely to justify the closure of a single one of the
schools that I saw in Herefordshire. If there is a problem with
heads, for instance, why not change the system? Renewable
tenure is one idea; appointment for a limited term of years is in
some ways a better one. It is perfectly possible to find a solution
to the problem. And so the question still remains unanswered.
Why are the school closures happening? Why are they happening *now*? And the answer, of course, is money. Many village
schools were closed in the 1950s as the all-age elementaries were
phased out. Then came a lull. The present crescendo of closures
is occurring not because the educational arguments are suddenly overwhelming, but because falling rolls at a time of economic crisis encourage the local authorities to shut down schools.
They feel obliged to do this in order to hold the rates as low as
possible while staying within government spending limits. Their
troubles are vastly increased by the low share of the rate
support grant awarded to the rural authorities. What we are
witnessing today is the deliberate destruction, as an economy
measure by local and central government combined, of one of
the few areas of British education that is genuinely working
well.

School size and sixth forms: A note

Parents like small secondary schools. Everyone agrees they do;
and this is probably true, even though there is nothing more to
prove it than anecdotal evidence. Despite attempts to provide
humane forms of internal organization, big schools are often

said to be impersonal. Certainly they look it, at least to an adult eye. Pupils don't seem to feel so strongly. In the course of writing a full-length profile of a 1500-strong London comprehensive, Hunter Davies conducted a survey of sixth formers.[15] He discovered that 90 per cent of them thought the size 'just right'. Only four said the school was too big. This suggests that the problem is not perhaps so serious as some parents believe. Nor are there quite so many big schools, either. There are fourteen comprehensives with over 2000 pupils, 231 with over 1500.[16] The average size is about 900.

One of the motives for having biggish comprehensives is to produce a sixth form large enough to justify the employment of the specialist teachers needed if a school is to offer a full range of academic subjects. Where sixth forms are small, subject choice is often limited; and teaching groups may be tiny. In 1976, 60 per cent of all classes with pupils aged sixteen or over had ten or fewer pupils. Of sixth-form modern language groups surveyed by the Inspectorate, 60 per cent had fewer than five pupils. The average staffing ratio in sixth forms was something like one to ten, better than many university departments.

To a government anxious for economies, this began to look horrendously expensive. From the point of view of cost and range of subject the D.E.S. calculated that sixth forms did not become workable till they had 140 or more pupils, 100 of them aiming for 'A' level. Yet 40 per cent of all comprehensive sixth forms had fewer than fifty pupils.

Early in 1977 Mrs Williams and other ministers began to speak in favour of sixth-form colleges, which would gather in all pupils over sixteen from the surrounding town or countryside. There were already seventy of these, with another twenty in the pipeline. They act essentially as sixth forms and nothing else. There is also another type of college – the so-called tertiary college or college of further education – offering both 'A' levels and vocational subjects within a more adult context (no school rules, etc). To many 'liberals' either sixth-form or, better still, tertiary colleges seemed to offer large advantages. Schools without sixth forms would be fairer, they argued. At present, there was glory for those who planned to stay on, a sense of failure for the majority who left at sixteen. Everyone would now have a chance to be in the top year. And the colleges, particularly the tertiary colleges with work-oriented courses, would be genuinely comprehensive.

To many head-teachers, however, the idea was anathema. The traditional sixth form was their crowning glory and their salaries were partly dependent on having one. Was all this now to be taken away, leaving behind impoverished eleven-to-sixteen schools unattractive both to teachers and to parents? A cry of grief ascended heavenwards.

Nor was it entirely clear that closing down the sixth forms would actually save money. 'Those who say that sixth forms, small though some may be, are uneconomic literally cannot know what they are saying,' wrote Mr Newsam of the I.L.E.A. in a letter to *The Times Educational Supplement*. He went on to demonstrate without much difficulty that a system of sixth-form colleges for Inner London would cost £2,400,000 a year. Wouldn't it be easier, he asked, to ensure that sixth forms cooperated pair by pair in having a common timetable, thus producing that 'epitome of economy, the 200-place sixth form'?

Perhaps surprised by so much indignation, the D.E.S. decided not to put out a circular that had been planned. This would have helped to boost the sixth-form colleges. Instead, discussions were to be held and a thorough analysis of costing undertaken. Temporarily, therefore, a lively issue went to sleep again. It will have to wake up soon. Sixth forms are still growing, but by the 1990s today's dearth of young children will cause numbers to plummet. The problem of viability will increase enormously.

Notes

1. Community Relations Commission 1975: *Participation of Ethnic Minorities in the General Election* (October 1974).
2. Select Committee on Race Relations and Migration, Session

1976/77 'The West Indian Community'. Evidence of Office of Population Census and Survey.

3. Little, A. N., *Educational Policies for Multi-Racial Areas* (Goldsmith's College, 1978).

4. Giles, Raymond, *The West Indian Experience in British Schools* (Heinemann, 1977). Though highly criticized on publication because of its anecdotal quality and polemical conclusions, this book is nevertheless full of shrewd perceptions.

5. Milner, David, *Education and Race* (Penguin Education, 1975). Confirmed by other sources.

6. Quoted in Little, A. N., *Educational Policies for Multi-Racial Areas* (Goldsmith's College, 1978).

7. *Funding Multi-Racial Education: a National Strategy* (Community Relations Commission, 1976).

8. The money is provided under Section 11 of the Local Government Act, 1966.

9. See Milner, and Giles, op. cit. notes 4 and 5 above.

10. There is a useful Runnymede Trust briefing paper on this subject – 'Billingualism and Linguistic Minorities in Britain – Developments, Perspectives', by Verity Saifullah Khan.

11. Little, A. N., *Educational Policies for Multi-Racial Areas* (Goldsmith's College, 1978).

12. Rutter, Michael, 'Children of West Indian Immigrants II: Intellectual performance and reading attainment', *Journal of Child Psychology and Psychiatry*, Vol. 16, 1975. Other numbers of the same journal carry work by Rutter on West Indians. His more general work on inner-city children is widely scattered through learned journals such as the *British Journal of Psychiatry* and the *Proceedings of the Royal Society of Medicine*. See also his general review of the literature – *Cycles of Disadvantage*, Rutter, Michael, and Madge, Nicola (Heinemann, 1976). I am grateful to Michael Marland, headmaster of Woodberry Down Comprehensive, for leading me to Rutter's work; and I would like to commend it warmly to any reader with a specialist interest.

13. Giles, Raymond, *The West Indian Experience in British Schools* (Heinemann, 1977).

14. *Where*, August 1976.

15. Davies, Hunter, *The Creighton Report* (Hamish Hamilton, 1976).

16. Statistical appendix, H.M.I. papers for York Conference on Comprehensive Education.

6. Where are we now?

The most notable consequence of the school debate so far has probably been the tightening up and rightward swing inside the schools. The government's declaration that school and industry must come together is an important change in principle. Apart from this, surprisingly little has altered noticeably to date. The only real events have been the publication of two documents. The first, in July 1977, was the government's consultative Green Paper *Education in Schools*. The second was the Taylor Report on governors and managers which finally appeared that September. *Education in Schools* contained little that was startling but led to much official consultation and to some activity at least. With Taylor it was the other way round. The proposals were radical but nothing seemed likely to happen. This chapter briefly assesses developments in each main area of the debate, up to March 1978, and offers a checklist for the future.

Curriculum

The possibility of sudden, crude changes to the curriculum seemed to have gone away for good. The idea of a tightly prescribed core was ruled out early, as we have seen. But in the Green Paper the government proposed a questionnaire to find out exactly what local authorities did and thought about the curriculum. The questions were evolved during the autumn and winter of 1977-8. Their tone implied that the authorities should take a much more interventionist line. What steps had the authority taken over this, that and the other, asked the D.E.S., with the implied extra question 'If none, why not?' Sometimes the extra question was actually asked. In this way, the local authorities were virtually told to exert themselves in ensuring a balanced curriculum, in checking on particular subjects, especially English, maths, science and modern languages, and also over continuity between schools, the records of pupils (a very important point), and links with local industry. It was as if the government, having seized the initiative and gathered power to itself, was now redistributing it – but anywhere except into the teachers' hands. The N.U.T., naturally, did not like this very much. The union feared that the knowledge the government would gain might provide a framework for intervention, and they particularly resented the question: 'What curriculum elements do the authority regard as essential?' This, they felt, could be the thin end of the common-core wedge. Accordingly the N.U.T. at first urged local authorities not to cooperate in filling in the questionnaire. To some this seemed an excessive reaction, for while the teachers might lose some of their power over the curriculum they could scarcely have it all taken away. The essence of teaching, after all, is the private transaction between teacher and pupil. This would remain whatever happened. *The Times Educational Supplement* was probably right when it predicted a long and shuffling process of readjustment between all the parties concerned.

In March 1978, hard on the heels of a report from the Institute of Mathematics which showed that vast numbers of school leavers were unable to cope with simple, everyday mathematical tasks, the government announced a major inquiry into the teaching of mathematics in school.

School and Work

The Green Paper preceded but chimed well with Mr Callaghan's assertion that it was the duty of the schools to boost the nation's economy by creating favourable attitudes to industry. Most people accepted this as proper. The government's proposal was for the economic life of the country to figure more largely in the curriculum and for a profusion of local and national contracts between school and the 'world of work'. Schemes run by the Schools Council and the C.B.I. received encouragement and plaudits. 'Special' industrial scholarships were mooted for degree students of exceptional ability. The government believed that all this would have the intended propaganda effect. It was widely regarded as unsporting to wonder whether closer acquaintance with industry might not the more effectively deter the young. But if this happened, the Callaghan project would fail and education would get the blame. Nor was there much evidence to suggest that production would improve even if attitudes did become more favourable. Education had so far failed to crack the class structure. Now it was being allocated another major social task which might prove equally intractable. Nevertheless, only the most foolish could contemplate the mutual ignorance of school and industry with equanimity. And it seemed that even if Mr Callaghan's greater goal was unattainable, both sides might benefit from better knowledge of one another.

For the young unemployed, there was now much greater provision, mostly in government-aided jobs and vocational courses. These have flowed from the Holland Report[1] of May 1977 which recommended expenditure of £168 million per year, with an annual 'throughput' of 230,000 young people. The government accepted these proposals and acted on them almost instantaneously. But because the D.E.S. cannot give specific grants, even the educational side of this project was handled by the fast-growing Manpower Services Commission. The M.S.C. scheme was ambitious and imaginative in concept. In practice, being a sudden expedient, it appeared somewhat confused. One of the worst problems was over the financial support the young unemployed would receive while studying. At £18 per week, this looked enough to attract many youngsters away from school or orthodox further education. This and other difficulties strengthened the feeling, both in education and among the trades unions, that the problems of sixteen- to nineteen-year-olds should be looked at as a whole. It seemed absurd to be talking about sixth forms and tertiary colleges inside the world of education while the Manpower Services Commission was making arrangements which might sabotage them both. Strong calls began to be heard for a fast-moving inquiry into the prospects for sixteen- to nineteen-year-olds, a matter likely to be resolved before this book is published.

Standards and Exams

The Labour party, previously presented by opponents as the butcher of the grammar schools, appeared to have gone a long way towards demonstrating that it was now a party of standards. This was probably one of Mr Callaghan's main intentions. But the Green Paper definitively ruled out, at least for the duration of the Labour government, any move towards national testing as envisaged by the Conservatives. Instead, the A.P.U., Her Majesty's Inspectorate and local authority advisers were all encouraged in their work. There was also encouragement for local authorities to do their own testing, preferably using standardized tests being prepared by the National Foundation for Educational Research. At the time of writing, the move towards local authority testing showed signs of turning into a stampede.

On public exams, Mrs Williams was expected soon to take over the decision whether or not to give the go-ahead to the Schools Council's sixteen-plus proposals. This was critically important. In early 1978 things began to look more favourable for the sixteen-plus. A group which had been mulling over the problems on Mrs Williams' behalf seemed to have found a solution to the administration of the new exam which would give more weight to the university-backed G.C.E. boards. As Mrs Williams was anxious to limit further growth of teacher power, this idea had obvious attraction. On the other hand, the imminence of a general election might make her reluctant to act in so controversial a matter. If this were so, then sixteen-plus reform would depend on a Labour victory.

The Schools Council received a new constitution. Nobody liked it very much but it met the government's requirements by putting an end to teacher-union majority at various vital points. As soon as the constitution was agreed Sir Alex Smith resigned, declaring that he had plenty on his plate in Manchester.

In languages, that great disaster zone, an interesting exam proposal had been made. This was for stage-by-stage testing as in music. It seemed a good idea and may turn out to have some mileage in the future.

The Teachers

The government wanted more black teachers and more with experience of industry. There was a lot of talk about this but no effective action up to March 1978. On the other hand, brisk and positive steps were taken on entry qualifications. It was decided that the last general entry for the non-graduate certificate courses would be in 1979–80 (with exceptions for entrants hoping to work in shortage subjects). By 1980–81 all students entering initial training would normally be expected to have the same qualifications as people starting a degree course. Possibly more important still, from September 1980 onwards trainees would be expected to have a G.C.E. 'O' level (grade C or above) or a C.S.E. Grade I in both mathematics and English. Failing this, they would have to show by some clear proof that they had reached the equivalent standard.

This held out some hope for maths in the far-distant future. But prospects seemed bleak when it came to improving the teaching of non-specialists already in the schools. Several knowledgeable and well-respected voices warned that short courses for the innumerate might actually increase confusion, giving the teachers half-baked ideas instead of none at all.

For induction and in-service training generally, the outlook was grim. But this remained an area where it still seemed just possible for a powerful policy initiative to be taken.

For newly trained teachers out of work, some opportunities were provided for retraining in shortage subjects.

The most controversial recommendation in the whole of the Green Paper dealt with bad teachers. After the customary genuflection to the general competence and goodwill of the profession, the Green Paper advocated retraining and sideways movement for the marginally incompetent. But to deal with 'the difficult residue of cases where no effective remedy presents itself' the government proposed consultations with the unions, so as to set up some recognized way of assessing, advising, warning and, where finally necessary, dismissing. The unions snarled at this. But discussions did begin. They remained unresolved at the time of writing.

Control

The Taylor report, as predicted, took the side of parents and the community. It said that governing bodies should be made up of four equal parts: local authority representatives, teachers, parents, and representatives of the community at large. They should have general power over the curriculum and even over some aspects of discipline. (The committee felt that suspension was over-used and that the governors should license and limit it.) Predictably, the outcry of the vested interests was instantaneous. The Taylor Committee had misused its opportunity, said Mr Jarvis for the N.U.T.: 'The net effect of their report is to prescribe a busybodies' charter and to hand over the running of schools to management by unaccountable committees.' The N.A.S./U.W.T. said Taylor proposed 'a bogus partnership', destructive of professional responsibility. Spokesmen for the local authorities were also extremely hostile. They feared that governing bodies with substantial teacher representation would be a fresh arena for the inter-union struggle. They feared that parents would side with teachers, doubling their power. They worried about the oddity of the folk who might emerge to represent the community, and they worried about loss of political patronage, even though the present political carve-up of governing bodies was sharply criticized by

Taylor. Even more important was the contradiction implied by any acceptance of Taylor. For just when the government seemed to be offering local authorities power by way of the curricular survey, Taylor was asking them to give it away again. Mrs Williams for her part attempted to wriggle out of this absurdity. What she wanted, she let it be known, was to include new blood on the governing bodies and only later to tackle the question of their powers. This was very much a politician's move, for it would gratify the public – if the public was innocent enough to be taken in – without threatening the power of the local authorities. In the end she achieved nothing because there was no parliamentary time available for her. This meant that the *status quo* would carry on. And the parents, of course, had no way of doing the slightest thing about it. Taylor had been buried alive by teachers and local authorities. It seemed, in short, that control would continue to be dispersed among all parties except the immediate users of the service – parents and children.

Inner Cities and Village Schools

Because of its lack of power to pay for projects, the D.E.S. did little to help the inner cities. Government funds under the Urban Programme were failing to reach the ethnic minorities. The situation would have been entirely grim if local authorities had not begun to embark on their own programmes, despite the great shortage of cash. But falling rolls meant serious difficulties for children and teachers in city and country alike. Despite public resentment, schools were beginning to close in the inner cities and were already closing fast in country villages. The government's contribution, in my view a malign one, was to issue a circular (5/77) calling on local authorities to be 'resolute' in the closure of under-used schools.

On the positive side the government picked up various proposals from the 1977 Select Committee report on immigration. This report had been a powerful force in drawing attention to the difficulties of West Indians; and one of its proposals had been the collection of reliable and useful statistics on the number and distribution of ethnic-minority school-children. The government now agreed, said the Green Paper, that statistical knowledge was 'essential for any effective policy of positive discrimination to help meet the special needs of ethnic minorities'. But discussions were to be held before any collection of statistics was embarked upon. This seemed a good idea in view of earlier failures to consult the minority groups about decisions which affected them; and, as we have seen, the idea of collecting statistics is highly controversial. There were also to be discussions about the idea of holding a high-level inquiry into the special problems of West Indians. Both sets of talks were still in progress in March 1978.

In conclusion, it would seem that on all the issues of the school debate there is still room for argument, aggravation and even, who knows, progress. If I am right in thinking that the biggest change of all has been in mood inside the schools, then will this mean the establishment of a new and healthy balance or have the floodgates of reaction been thrown open? Will the schools agree to serve the aims of industry? Will the teachers succeed in their assertion that only they should have responsibility for what is taught? Will parents have to go on crying in the wilderness? These are some of the questions I would ask in assessing each future development.

Note

1. *Young People and Work*, Manpower Services Commission, 1977.

Index

More About Penguins and Pelicans

Penguinews, which appears every month, contains details of all the new books issued by Penguins as they are published. From time to time it is supplemented by our stocklist, which includes around 5,000 titles.

A specimen copy of *Penguinews* will be sent to you free on request. Please write to Dept EP, Penguin Books Ltd, Harmondsworth, Middlesex, for your copy.

In the U.S.A.: For a complete list of books available from Penguins in the United States write to Dept CS, Penguin Books, 625 Madison Avenue, New York, New York 10022.

In Canada: For a complete list of books available from Penguins in Canada write to Penguin Books Canada Ltd, 2801 John Street, Markham, Ontario L3R 1B4

Some recent and forthcoming Pelicans

Seven Years Old in the Home Environment

John and Elizabeth Newson

This third volume in the Newsons' seminal study of child up bringing investigates some seven hundred Nottingham children at a critical stage in their development. In transition from infant to junior school, they are moving out of the protective family orbit and into the wider social world of street, playground and classroom.

Like the earlier books, this report has a strong ecological flavour. The motives and actions of both parents and children are firmly set in the broader context of contemporary urban society; the authors present an impressive structure of hard factual data, while putting flesh on statistical bones by constant reference to parents' own thoughts and reactions, recorded in their own words. The result is a rich description of seven-year-olds and their world.

The Arabs

Peter Mansfield

Peter Mansfield's authoritative study is the product of considerable research and a deep understanding of the Arab world. Beginning with the nomads of Arabia, this historical survey documents the life of Muhammad and the rise of the Islamic empire, through to the period of western colonialism and Arab nationalism, concluding with the modern Arab renaissance reinforced by oil power. An important section of the book covers the Arab states in gazetteer fashion, and the final part deals with the current Arab situation and their aspirations for the future.

'a masterly survey . . . Mr Mansfield's book can show us the way' – Edward Mortimer in *The Times*

Two forthcoming Pelicans on education

A Guide to Learning After School
Michael Locke and John Pratt

Here is a guide to the varied sources of post-school education: further and higher education provided by local authorities; the universities; industrial training offered by employers, training boards and government agencies; evening classes; and correspondence colleges and other private and charitable institutions. It tells you how to find out about a course, be it in basic cookery, welding or astral physics, what qualifications you will need, how to apply for a grant (if relevant), what your rights are, and how to complain if you don't get them.

Teaching Thinking
Edward de Bono

Can children be taught to think – not think *about* things, but to think as a specific skill? And if they can, does it really do them any good?

Edward de Bono has done more than any other man to bring the concept of 'thinking' into the real world. Now he has devised a programme for the teaching of thinking within the framework of the school timetable, and it is already being used by some two million children of all ages and abilities. It is set out here.

'One of the best educational books that I have ever met' – Martyn Berry in *New Scientist* a Penguin Education Special coming soon:

The Condition of English Schooling

Edited by Henry Pluckrose and Peter Wilby

In the mid-1970s, education became the theme of a hot debate when the problems of the William Tyndale school hit the headlines. In the autumn of 1976 a small group of people from all walks of life and representing no fixed political or commercial interests met to discuss ways in which the 'Great Debate' could be put to more constructive use. They all agreed to produce this book.

The wide variety of views collected here come from teachers, parents, schoolchildren, MPs, local authority administrators, journalists, lecturers and prospective employers. They reflect different attitudes to, and experiences of, the various facets of modern education. Some are concerned with theory and principles, others with practice and pragmatism. All are anxious to fill in some of the gaps in the current debate on this vital issue.

Designed deliberately to show the complexity of the problem, *The Condition of English Schooling* does not pretend to be a blueprint for the future. What it does offer is a valuable exposition of the situation today, which we need to understand before we can even consider tomorrow.

Penguin Education

Colleges in Crisis
David Hencke

'The history of teacher education over the last 180 years shows that even after the drastic changes of the last five years it is still, in 1978, in the confused state it was in 1798 . . . The planning of the teacher training system for the next decade is still unclear. The political machinery of modern government has failed to provide a rational solution to its problems.'

The upheaval in teacher training over the last few years has entailed the closure of some fifty institutions, mergers among many others, and created a new group of institutions, the colleges of higher education. What was the purpose of the reorganization? Why did so many newly trained teachers leave the colleges only to join the dole queue when the predicted expansion in teaching posts failed to materialize?

David Hencke followed the events described in *Colleges in Crisis* and was able to discuss them with teachers, college principals, lecturers and members of the James Committee. His account of the government reports, the arguments between policy-makers and educationists, and ways in which the colleges reacted to the call to reorganize is full, clear and well-documented. Everyone concerned about teacher training in this country will want to read it.